Encouraging Appropriate Behaviour

A Six-Step Approach

Murray Irwin

CENTENNIAL

Centennial

First published 2012 for Savi Consulting Pty Ltd
by Centennial, a division of
Publish-Me!
68 Oxford Street
Woollahra NSW 2025 Australia
www.publish-me.com.au
info@publish-me.com.au
T. +61 2 9362 8441

National Library of Australia Cataloguing-in-Publication entry

Author: Irwin, Murray.
Title: Encouraging appropriate behaviour : a six-step guide / Murray Irwin.
ISBN: 9780987227805 (pbk.)
Subjects: Behavior modification.
            Discipline of children.
            Problem solving with children.
            Interpersonal relations in children.
Dewey Number: 649.64

Acknowledgements

Thanks to Bernie, Beth, Bob, Carol, Charlie, Sam, Sophie and Suz for your comments and suggestions on my early drafts. Special thanks to Suz, who has given me great inspiration and insights and helped when this project was nothing more than a few training manual pages.

This book would never have been written had I not worked alongside a fantastic group of great people from whom I learnt to apply many of the ideas listed in this book. Working at Typo Station was a significant part of those experiences, and would not have existed without the inspiration and determination of its founder, Matt Phahlert. Thanks to Matt and of course all the Typo staff, volunteers and supporters. Not only did they pave the way before me, but they supported me while I worked there. It was a life-changing experience, not only for the young men who attended the residential program but for all the staff as well.

Thanks to the Publish-Me! team David, Lucie, Siobhan, Sebastian, Carol, Vanessa and Simon who helped bring this book to publication.

I hope this book will help provide you with ideas that will make a positive difference in your own and other people's lives.

Murray

IChing Hexagram 42 -
Increasing

*So the wise note the ways of others.
If they see good in others, they
imitate it. If they see bad in
themselves, they remove it.*

Disclaimer

The aim of this book is to provide information relating to the management of behaviour in a variety of general settings, situations and circumstances. The informaton is intended only as a guide and does not replace appropriate professional training and adherence to ethical, professional and legal standards.

It is important to note that some behaviours may be the result of psychological or pshychiatric illness. If mental health is a concern, seek the assistance from an appropriately qualified mental health professional. Special care needs to be taken in situations where aggressive and violent behaviour occurs or is threatened. Seek help from appropriate services and professionals.

The author and the publisher accept no responsibility or liability for the actions of any person who uses the information in this book. Any use of the information provided is at your own risk. This book is sold with the understanding that the author and publisher are not engaged in providing psychological or counselling services.

Many examples used in this book derive from actual events, therefore, names and some details have been altered to protect the privacy of those involved.

Contents

Introduction

When I first began as a youth worker, I was fascinated by human behaviour – why we did things and how we could sometimes be the cause of our own undoing. A high priority was helping others find more appropriate ways to meet their needs and goals. This was because much of the trouble and unhappiness currently in their lives was due to behaviour that was inappropriate for the situation.

Inappropriate behaviour is a general term used throughout this book to describe behaviour that fails any of the following:

- effectively communicate the issue or need
- respect others
- ensure the rights of all parties
- meet the agreed expectations, agreements or laws of a group or community
- be consistently applied.

Appropriate behaviour ensures that all five of the above aspects of behaviour are present.

When I began researching for tools and strategies the amount of knowledge and information available was overwhelming. But there appeared to be a gap when I looked for a practical introduction to encouraging behaviour change. There were two major barriers that I felt needed to be overcome:

1. Theory. Much of the information was theoretical and needed to be adapted to apply its use in a practical manner.
2. Framework. I could not find a framework to bring all the tools together that would help determine the best strategies to use, based on the individual circumstances.

In the end, the majority of what I learnt was from those with whom I had worked. As with any profession, it can take years of trial and error to refine the use of various techniques. And, once accomplished, we absorb the processes, doing them automatically without thinking. Upon realising that I was no longer consciously thinking about what I did and how I responded, I set about trying to understand what I was unconsciously doing. The goal was to determine how best to pass that information onto others.

So, I developed my own process to help provide a framework – the six step BECOME process. BECOME stands for behaviour, emergency, context, options, myself and enact. Using this, I have been able to identify the principles, tools and strategies that are arguably the most important. And, by using the knowledge that was hard earned by the many helping professionals before me, I can now say I consciously understand what it is that I do when grappling with behavioural challenges.

There are many books that address specific problems or diagnoses, such as anger management or attention deficit hyperactivity disorder (ADHD). They generally offer advice for handling very specific situations. This book is geared more towards handling overall inappropriate behaviour that is not tied to a specific diagnosis, disorder or problem. These behaviours occur simply because the person exhibiting it is attempting to fill a need and does not know or has not learned a more constructive way to do so.

This book is a guide to help replace inappropriate behaviour with appropriate behaviour. Although this approach is based on my experiences working with adolescents, it can be applied to individuals of almost any age and maturity level.

I have strived to use plain English and easy-to-understand concepts to demonstrate how to:

1. constructively respond to inappropriate behaviour,
2. quickly identify the most effective tools to use when responding, and
3. effectively share these techniques with others who are in a position to support the process of change.

How this book is structured

Chapters one through four provide the foundation information for the six steps, identified by the acronym, BECOME. Chapter one overviews the six steps as well as defining what principles, tools and strategies are. Chapter two discusses the foundations, including core values and most of the underlying principles. Chapter three looks at agreements and what should be contained in a behaviour agreement and how to most effectively use it. Chapter four reviews key communication tools as well as exploring aggression.

Chapters five through ten each cover one of the six BECOME steps. The Behaviour and Emergency Assessment steps focus on what is the behaviour. Context explores why the person is behaving in that manner and when it occurs. The Options, Myself and the Enact steps, help determine how to best encourage changing the behaviour to something that is appropriate.

Each BECOME step is explored in detail, with a short scenario to illustrate the need for that step. Both an aim (or goal) and action (response) is provided. The key principles behind each step are then discussed, followed by the appropriate tools to use. Within each tool is a section entitled 'in practice', which describes the execution of the step using the particular tool in more detail.

Chapter eleven discusses a range of strategies on how to support the changes in various circumstances. In chapter twelve, a case study featuring the fictitious students, Jessie and Harley, is examined, taking you through each step of the BECOME behavioural management technique to illustrate how to implement it. This discusses the process, how the principles help, the ways tools can be used, and, finally, the use of strategies.

The appendix contains a blank worksheet for you to reproduce and use. The worksheet can act as a memory aid or, if required, to record details. A summary of the 'Jessie and Harley' case study is provided on sample worksheets. Also included is additional information that supports the tools used.

Who will benefit from this book

This book was written to help anyone deal with situations where inappropriate behaviour occurs. There are a number of specific groups who should find this book particularly useful. They include youth group leaders, counsellors, education professionals, parents, and humanities students.

Scout and Guide leaders, sport coaches, camp leaders, mentors, and other youth group leaders will find the techniques outlined in this book helpful, particularly those serving in a voluntary capacity who do not have access to training or support. For more experienced leaders, this book offers the opportunity to reflect on your practice and offers strategies to consider during those difficult situations where you find yourself unable to move forward in a positive manner.

Counsellors may wish to use the outlined approach in their own practice. For your clients needing to develop skills to deal with difficult behaviour, this book can be a resource in that process. It can also be beneficial when discussing client issues with other practitioners and/or client support networks.

This book offers a way in which education professionals may discuss student behaviour with parents and highlight strategies that have and have not worked. For those teaching humanities or building student skills, the approach and tools in this book can form a resource to use in classroom teaching. Administrators will find that this approach supports having a consistent, whole school approach to behaviour management.

Parents can more objectively review the behaviour of their children using these techniques. The tools and strategies contained here will help develop social skills in their children, to enable them to become happy, healthy, and successful adults. This book also offers a way in which any behavioural difficulties can be discussed with others in the child's support network, including teachers, coaches, relatives and friends. This ensures that all of the child's support networks are approaching the behaviour consistently and supportively.

Students studying psychology, behaviour and related humanities subjects or services will find this book useful in learning about putting behaviour theory into practice.

Conventions used in this book

In an effort to make this book easier to use, when a specifically defined principle, tool or strategy is mentioned, subsequent to its definition, an abbreviation will appear in brackets following the reference, i.e., [P] for principle, [T] for tool and [S] for strategy. In addition, some technical terms and concepts that have specific meaning in psychology have been replaced with lay explanations in plain English. For those wishing to do further research using academic or technical sources, the technical terms may sometimes be provided in brackets.

In order to recognise sources of information, the American Psychological Association (APA) standard for citation has been used. This provides the author(s) and date of the publication. Complete details of the source can be found in the reference section.

To avoid complicating illustrative examples with gender-oriented identification, whenever possible, gender neutral first names and terms have been used.

Limitations of this book

No book can foresee and/or adequately address every possible situation that might arise. However, the steps in this book will organise your approach to every situation so that you can address each in a thoughtful way. Experience and practice will develop the necessary skills to deal with all manner of different problems using this process. Ideally, it will reduce the learning curve and the time required to solve the problem.

Please be aware that many of the tools and strategies assume a certain ability (cognitive development) on the part of the recipient to understand concepts, such as mutual respect. In situations involving very young children, people with developmental disorders, and those suffering psychological or psychiatric disorders, the tools and strategies in this book may not always prove useful or appropriate. In such instances, it is recommended that referral be made to an appropriately qualified professional for assistance.

Special care must be taken where aggression or violence is threatened or present. Again, appropriate assistance and qualified professional advice should be sought.

Chapter one

The six-step process for encouraging appropriate behaviour

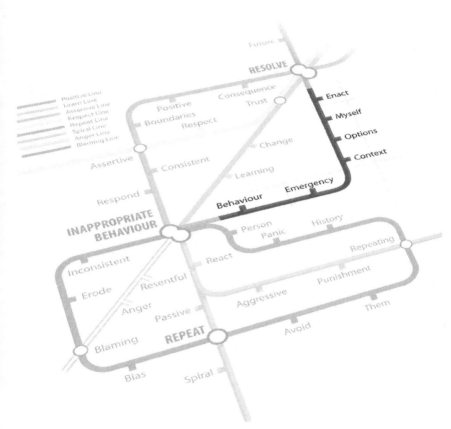

The six-step process is designed to:

- assess behaviour and the context in which it occurs,
- assist you to make an informed decision about the most appropriate action to gain a positive solution,
- guide you in implementing the action, and
- aid you in subsequently evaluating how effective the action was.

Similar to a medical emergency, it is beneficial to have a structured step-by-step approach to dealing with behavioural issues. For example, first aid courses teach the DR ABC model (danger, response, airway, breathing and circulation). Having steps to follow, especially in times of great stress or high emotion, enables us better to remember what we need to do. It also helps provide a consistent approach and reduce the emotional biases to which we all are susceptible.

The six steps are identified via the acronym BECOME to make them easy to remember and to ensure no step is missed. A behavioural issue can 'BECOME' an opportunity for the person to learn and improve through an effective response.

The six steps are:

- **B – Behaviour**
  Step 1: identify the behaviour so you can clearly explain to the person what the behaviour is, the impact it has on others, and why it is considered inappropriate.

- **E – Emergency**
  Step 2: complete an emergency assessment to determine the danger or risks involved, in order to keep everyone safe.

- **C – Context**
  Step 3: review the context of the situation to see what situational factors and history might contribute to the behaviour.

- **O – Options**
  Step 4: begin formulating a response plan and decide on the most appropriate style of response. (There are 10 possible options for response styles to choose from in the response curve tool on page 82.)

- **M – Myself**
  Step 5: maintain self-awareness of our own feelings and what might be influencing our decision-making. We also need to understand how we might be part of the context creating the situation.

- **E – Enact**
  Step 6: enact the response. We need to take action otherwise nothing will change. Based on the response style, this is fine-tuned with a large range of possible strategies provided.

Implementing these six steps:

- creates a structure that gives you confidence to address issues
- helps maintain a calm and consistent approach when confronted with situations that can otherwise cause heightened emotions
- allows you to easily remember the process
- clarifies the situation objectively
- permits you to choose where to focus your energy, based on the varying circumstances
- generates new ideas and possibilities to explore as you address each step
- allows quick and simple analysis of situations.

Each of the six BECOME steps discussed in this book is accompanied by a set of supporting principles [P], tools [T], and suggested strategies [S]. To help explain concepts, each step includes a short scenario to help highlight key points. A full case study in chapter twelve (see page 122) is provided to illustrate the whole process in action. Also, there are easy-to-use worksheets and checklists supplied in the appendices.

Principles – how to approach inappropriate behaviour

These principles are generally accepted rules to work by and ways to approach a situation. The principles offered in this book are based on a solutions-focused approach.

Having and understanding relevant principles to follow:

- helps you avoid pitfalls
- arms you with vital insights
- builds your self confidence to handle situations effectively.

Tools – how to understand the situation

Tools are designed for you to gather information that will form the foundation of your decision-making. All the tools provide practical help to understand the behaviour or the context of the situation and implement an appropriate strategy.

Having a range of tools to use:

- can change your perception about problem behaviour
- reveals other possibilities and perspectives and gives you new insights
- helps you display and model assertive behaviour
- builds your knowledge and understanding about the behaviour.

Strategies – how to support change

Strategy in this context is the action taken to address the behaviour – the 'I will now do this' action. An obvious strategy may present itself as you address the situation, however, a range of possible strategies is provided to accommodate varying circumstances. These examples can help broaden the response so that it does not become repetitive, mechanical or predictable.

Providing a range of possible strategies:

- allows you to create new ways of dealing with issues
- empowers you by extending your response repertoire
- gives you powerful options for taking charge of situations.

Strategies checklist – potential strategies

The strategies checklist provides a quick ready reference to various useful strategies. It can help supplement the BECOME worksheet to maintain comprehensive records of strategies used and as a tool for reflection.

Worksheets – help to document the process

The BECOME worksheet acts as a summary and prompt, allowing you to record pertinent information such as incident details. You can also note successful strategies to share and brainstorm possible solutions. The worksheet is a handy memory jogger, written record, summary and reflection tool.

Self-Awareness checklist – encouraging reflection

This checklist provides reflective questions about your personal impact on the situation and ability to create change. It is used in the 'M' (Myself) step.

Having worksheets and checklists:

- offers an easy reminder of the step-by-step process
- provides a timesaving way to record incidents when required
- allows a concise way to transfer information between practitioners
- guides self-reflection on the responses used
- helps to clarify issues.

Using BECOME

You may wonder if there will be enough time to proceed through all the steps. If you have to consciously and methodically go through each of the steps, assess the principles and use all of the tools, it could be too late to act. Especially when faced with an emergency situation. Like any skill, mastering these steps will take time, however, once learnt, they will become instinctive.

The conscious processing of all the various factors can be as rapid as a normal reaction you might have now. This is because many of the tools offered simply formalise what most of us currently do unconsciously.

Reflection is critical to your success. There is a lot to be learnt from reflecting on what actions were taken, regardless of the level of success achieved. Using the process as a guide for reflection will help you in the future by reinforcing what has and has not proved effective. In particular, reflection allows us to work out why a particular approach did not work. Reviewing the situation with a framework can be just as enlightening as using it during the event, because reflection lacks the element of stress that exists during a problem situation and allows you to think more calmly, clearly and methodically.

Chapter two

Foundations for supporting appropriate behaviour

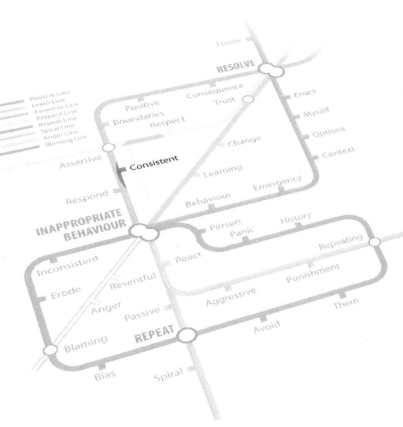

Before getting into the details of the six-step BECOME process, there are a number of ideas and tools that you need to be aware of that form the basic foundation of how to address inappropriate behaviour.

Core values

Values are the enduring beliefs you have about the patterns or modes of behaviour considered desirable or socially acceptable. You use values to help make decisions as they help form your attitudes and behaviours. The three core values considered important in working with the behaviour of others are:

1. strengths
2. solutions
3. fairness

Strengths

Everyone has strengths. These are talents we possess in particular areas, which we define as being good at something. However, when inappropriate behaviour is displayed, it can divert your attention and make you overlook or forget these strengths in others. The person you are focusing upon is the expert on what is happening in their life. Look for and utilise those strengths to help develop solutions.

Solutions

We must think first about what would be happening at that moment if the problem had not presented itself. This will lead to a solution. It moves the focus from the problem to how best to support a solution.

Fairness

Fairness is treating everyone the same and uses the processes of restorative justice. It requires us first to hear what happened from every party involved. How everyone has been affected by an action, and then to hear what might be done to improve the situation. Restorative justice avoids the use of punishment or power while still requiring everyone to take responsibility for their behaviour (The Victorian Association for Restorative Justice, 2011).

You may already be familiar with the background to these three core values. However, a detailed understanding is not required when working through the BECOME steps, as they have been embedded in the practices throughout.

Underlying principles

Principles help guide you when approaching a situation. There are seven underlying principles that are relevant to all parts of the BECOME framework. (There are other principles that are important to specific steps and these are discussed within the relevant steps.) Principles are like prerequisites for good practice. These seven underlying principles are:

1. unconditional positive regard
2. being a positive role model
3. establishing and ensuring consistency
4. responding versus reacting
5. swapping, not stopping
6. converting problem behaviour into skill-based behaviour
7. providing justification

Unconditional positive regard

Unconditional positive regard is when you demonstrate a 'complete, non-judgemental acceptance of the client as a person' and to 'value the client as a human being,' (Weiten, 1998, p. 610). It is about maintaining a positive outlook towards a person and maintaining basic respect for them, despite any undesirable behaviour.

Unconditional positive regard underlies why it is so important to separate the behaviour from the person. If that person acted appropriately, we would have no issue with them and would exhibit positive regard towards them. But to exhibit that positive regard only when they act appropriately creates an unstable relationship as it fluctuates, swinging back and forth like a pendulum between the positive and the negative. Why would they respect or listen to you if you fail to offer them basic respect? Or if you only offer it conditionally, depending on their actions.

It does not mean you approve of the behaviour, but it shows that you accept them as a person. Ask yourself, if that behaviour were not present, whether your acceptance of them would be different at that moment? Approach the situation by having basic respect for the person independent of their behaviour.

Being a positive role model

One of the most effective ways to encourage good behaviour in others is to teach by example. Given that most of our learning may come from watching others (observational learning), it is important that you demonstrate the right behaviours. If you are to support others' change, knowing and showing the appropriate behaviour ourselves is critical to success.

There are three key factors to effective role modelling. The first, as discussed above, is behaving appropriately. The next is that you act consistently. Consistency is of such importance this is considered a separate principle and is discussed below. The third factor is that your behaviour is congruent so it demonstrates by example.

If somebody was verbally abusing someone else and you intervened by verbally abusing the perpetrator, you have not been congruent. You know verbal abuse is wrong but you used the same technique when intervening. You are modelling the precise behaviour you have demanded they stop! Being congruent means acting in harmony with what you are trying to achieve. Apt, in agreement or fitting are other descriptors of being congruent.

You need to behave consistently and as you expect others to behave. There are four key points to achieving congruency:

- doing as you expect others to do
- role modelling congruent communication
- living as your word
- being true to yourself.

Doing as you expect others to do

If you expect certain behaviours from others, then lead by example and role model those behaviours. This means one rule for everyone. Consider congruency as the opposite of 'Do as I say, not as I do'. This is an area where the sense of injustice can be readily inflamed. If someone is required to act a certain way only to see others, especially authority figures, behave differently, this will inevitably generate feelings of unfairness and accusations of double standards.

There will be obvious exceptions to leading by example, especially when adolescents are involved. Adhering to the legal age to drink alcohol is an example. Be aware that even though such legal rules exist that you live by, it can still appear to adolescents that you are incongruent. Scolding adolescents for drinking alcohol when role models drink can send a mixed message. While role models are acting within the law, young people will want and are encouraged to emulate their role models.

You can address this through sound and valid reasoning to support the differences. The legal argument in the above case is sufficient but can easily be strengthened with reasoning based on the negative health impacts for brain development by drinking alcohol during adolescence. However, if someone is trying to encourage responsible drinking among adults and role models the use of alcohol irresponsibly, then it would be harder to establish a congruent reason. The expectation would be to lead by example. The more congruent you are, the more respect and trust you will build. And the easier life will be as you do not have to constantly justify perceived inconsistencies.

Role modelling congruent communication

When dealing with others the way you communicate using body language, words and tone generally needs to be congruent. (This is also discussed in the section on communication channels in chapter four, see page 31.) For example, saying that there is nothing to worry about when your manner and tone indicate that you are feeling really worried. This sends mixed signals. The game is already up as they know something is going on from your body language.

It is possible to remain congruent without divulging everything that is going on. Saying, 'Yes, I have a problem but I don't want to discuss it right now,' or 'I am working on solving it so you don't have to worry about it,' is far better because it is honest. There is acknowledgement of the problem and your body language matches the communication, therefore being congruent.

Living as your word

Being congruent also means following through on your promises. This is known as 'living as your word'. You must follow through with any agreements, rewards or consequences that you arrange, offered or propose. Therefore do not arrange, offer or propose something that you cannot, are not or will not be able to follow through on.

Failing to follow through will be exploited and could establish a pattern of behaviour that was not intended. If someone knowingly agrees to something that they cannot deliver, many consider this to be a lie. It follows that we begin to naturally question the reliability of other things that person says, undermining trust. So it is really important to think and plan ahead as to what you can and cannot do, what you will and will not do.

Being true to yourself

It is important to note that a parallel process is also occurring. That is the need for you to be yourself and be real, not construct some personality that does not align with your true nature. This is about being true to yourself. It is easy to see when people are not following their own beliefs or using styles with which they are not comfortable. The challenge is to be consistent with your own self, your personality and your values, and also to be consistent with the expected rules, agreements and norms that affect our daily lives.

Approach situations by doing as you expect others to do, ensuring your communication is congruent, living as your word and being true to yourself. Everyone will know when you are doing so, as congruency shines through.

Establishing and ensuring consistency

As discussed above, nothing inflames a sense of injustice more than when a rule is applied to one person and not to another, or when a rule is inconsistently enforced.

If this is the case when you are addressing unacceptable behaviour, it can steer the focus away from the unacceptable behaviour. Instead the focus becomes how you are administering the standards of behaviour. If you have been inconsistent, you now are in the position of having to defend yourself and to justify your actions. You must consistently apply all rules and standards to everyone involved, without exception.

If you do not, the natural instinct will be to continue testing the boundaries you have set. This occurs frequently with children and adolescents and you cannot blame them for this. They cannot question your fairness if you consistently provide a structured environment where everyone knows the rules and adheres to them. Consistently applying the boundaries establishes them as the norm and the testing of them lessens.

Lack of consistency provides fertile ground for undermining the implementation of the established norms and rules. If parents, for example, undermine each other's authority by being inconsistent, it is common for a child or adolescent to then play one parent against the other. This leads to a further lack of consistency. It creates issues and doubts between those attempting to apply the rules. Have no doubt about it – children, adolescents and adults are all very capable of exploiting inconsistencies to their own benefit.

It is important to establish the boundaries and norms from the very beginning, ideally before any inappropriate behaviour occurs or at the first occurrence. Ignoring it a few times before taking firm action is inconsistent. If this happens, the person legitimately does not know where the true boundary is. Immediate guidance from the very start is the best and quickest way to steer people away from disobeying the rules.

Consistency means applying the same rules to every situation with everybody. If there are any exceptions, stating them up front will help offset any resentment, as long as there is a credible reason for making such an exception. It could be that an older child can stay up later while the younger child has a different bedtime. Or you might not use a specific consequence for crossing out of the school playground boundary for a new student who did not know an area was outside the boundary. In making the exception ensure others know the reasons why, so they do not begin to think that they too, will receive the same exception.

Responding versus reacting

Many of us react to situations without conscious thought. Applying the six steps to deal with these situations requires bringing those processes from the unconscious to conscious. Doing so will help to more clearly describe the strategy you used, the situation, the reasoning and the outcome. This is of particular benefit when your strategy is being communicated or transferred to others.

The terms 'reacting' and 'responding' are used throughout this book to illustrate the difference between something done instinctively (reacting) and when a planned action with a clearly thought out objective has been implemented (responding). The goal is to create a mental habit from which you can move from reacting spontaneously to a situation without advance planning or forethought to responding thoughtfully. Knee-jerk reactions are where mistakes are most often made. A conscious, thoughtful response will more likely improve a situation than inflame it.

The following diagram illustrates the situation.

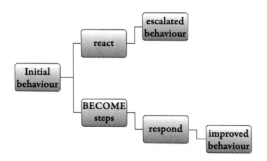

Responding versus reacting

Swapping, not stopping

This principle encourages replacing negative behaviour with an alternative positive behaviour, instead of merely demanding that the undesirable behaviour cease outright. In its most basic sense, all behaviour is driven by need, whether it is seeking food and water or protecting oneself from harm. (This is discussed further in the context step, see Chapter seven.) Wanting attention in and of itself is not a bad thing, but what the individual does to draw that attention can vary greatly.

This is why it is so difficult to simply discontinue certain types of behaviour without replacing them with constructive alternatives. The drive to satisfy a need is not quelled just because someone tells us we should not do something that was designed to fulfil that need. When we fail in one way to meet a need, we typically persist by exploring other ways to meet it. If you stop a behaviour and the need remains unmet, you must logically expect a different behaviour to occur to express that yet unfulfilled need.

Sometimes the need itself is inappropriate or cannot be filled. Then swapping will have to become stopping. We all have to learn to accept that we cannot always get what we want or need.

This principle is about how to approach situations by identifying what we can change to make this situation acceptable. If you were to replace the offending behaviour with something more positive, what would it be?

Converting problems into skills

This principle is particularly appropriate when working with younger children to resolve child developmental issues. It is based on the theory that issues confronting a child are best resolved by having the child learn a specific skill they currently lack. When the skill is acquired, the problem is resolved (Furman, 2004). For example, let's say that a child yells at others. If you were to approach this from the perspective that yelling is a problem that must be stopped, then you will tell the child that the yelling has to stop. However, by focusing on ending the problem by developing a skill, you would focus on teaching the child to instead talk quietly with the promise of being heard. You have provided another outlet, another skill in which the child can, in this case, meet the need to be heard.

We can view the behaviour of individuals, no matter what their age, using this approach because even in adulthood there can exist insufficient development of some skills. Helping to build skills to resolve problem behaviour is far more positive and constructive. Discussing it as 'improving a skill' helps the listener understand what needs to change without creating resentment. Ideally, it can be linked to the individual's existing skills and strengths. As in all conflict resolution, it is easier to create a willingness to change if the feedback and coaching is expressed in a positive manner.

Approach situations by focusing away from the problem and towards a positive action. This offers another way to view the situation that will help you to discover solutions together.

Providing justification

Whenever intervening because of inappropriate behaviour, it is vital that you do so for a legitimate reason. That reason needs to be valid and explainable. If you are unable to justify your intervention, why should individuals change their behaviour? It is not really appropriate to intervene if you cannot justify it in a manner that a reasonable person would consider acceptable.

'Because I said so,' may work in the short term, but it lacks credibility. Having a sound and valid explanation will help maintain boundaries. (Chapter three discusses this in more detail. See page

25.) Having reasons helps you to reflect on whether your request is really justified. Maybe it is the rules that need to change, not everyone's behaviour.

Be cautious when considering your justification. We have our own preferred way of how things should be. We should not confuse our preferred way with being the best, most valid or only way of completing things. Just because it is not our way of doing things does not automatically justify us to impose our way on others. Having an agreement on what is acceptable will provide the clues as to the justification.

Always approach situations ensuring you can provide a valid reason for the request.

Chapter three
Establishing agreement of what is appropriate behaviour

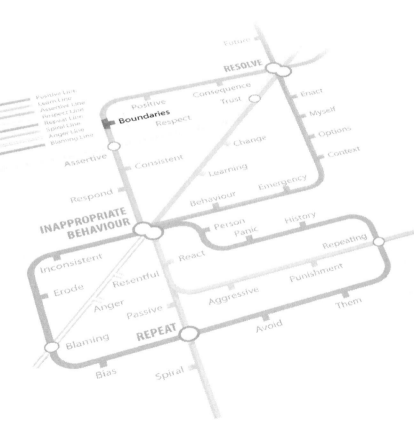

Aim	Clarify what is appropriate versus inappropriate behaviour.
Action	Use the agreement(s) to guide behaviour.

In Practice

Agreements form an essential tool in encouraging positive behaviour.

Agreements are contracts, whether written, verbal or merely implied, that establish modes of behaviour, rules and/or boundaries between parties. When established to regulate social settings, they can also be known as 'Full Value Contracts' (Schoel, Prouty and Radcliffe, 1988). This implies that they will help everyone get the most value out of their experiences and interactions.

Ideally, when a person is first introduced into your environment, you will establish some form of an agreement of what is deemed acceptable behaviour. Taking this step immediately lays the groundwork for consistency and justification and introduces the expectation of mutual respect between all parties. Without it, they will attempt to excuse their behaviour as stemming from ignorance of the rules (Luckner and Nadler, 1997). It also helps set the stage for authority figures to demonstrate positive role modelling, by personally following the same rules.

In most cases it is never to late to do something. Agreements fit this category and, if a formal agreement is not in place, then consider implementing one. It is important to do this in a collaborative manner and discuss the content before finalising the agreement. Forcing an agreement onto people when one did not previously exist can result in it being viewed with suspicion, fear, negativity and resistance. While facilitating input during implementation is necessary, it is important first to consider what your expectations are.

When created together with the individual or group, it helps everyone takes ownership of the agreement. Start a conversation with something like 'I would like to get input from (each of) you on what you see as the expectations for living/working in this group that we currently take for granted.'

A more direct approach is asking 'What rules do you think we need to help us live/work together successful and happily?'

Where collaboration is not possible, then a discussion should still be held regarding the content of the rules already established and the reasons behind them. The individuals should be granted the opportunity to discuss the meaning of items to ensure full understanding of your expectations.

Stating 'Because I said so,' as your reason does not help people understand why the rules are in place. There is no real justification given except a show of power. This creates a power play with the rule maker having power over the person or group. It now turns every issue into a contest for power rather than conforming to a set of rules that provides the best outcome for the family/group/ community as a whole. Rules should be impersonal and not attached to any one person or personality to avoid this type of power play situation.

A good agreement needs to be:

- **Positively framed** as much as possible. You want to describe what you want to create, not what you do not want. This helps provide a positive vision in order to create a willingness among the participants. For example, stating '...show respect for each other' is preferable to stating '...will not show disrespect for each other.'
- **Be broad and not too specific.** Use concepts like 'respect', 'feedback', and 'follow safety guidelines'. To attempt to describe every single action that can or cannot be done will create a list so long it will be unusable and no one will remember it. You will never be able to cover every possible circumstance that can occur so do not try. Opportunities to discuss the concepts help explain the agreement. For example, discuss how to show others respect.
- There may be **certain types of negative behaviour(s)** likely to occur that are essential to address specifically, such as violent behaviour or drug use. Include them by all means but make sure that they are kept to as few a number as possible. This could be captured in a sentence like,

'...will not engage in unlawful behaviour' or more positively framed as, '... will only engage in lawful behaviour'.

- **Consequences** when failing to comply with the agreement should also be included. These will need to be real consequences. That means they are realistic, justifiable, defined and, of course, you need to be willing and able to carry out the consequences. It is useless to make empty threats because your credibility will be shattered when your bluff is called and you fail to implement what the agreement said you would.

- Whenever possible, include the words, '**agreed to by the participants**'. This creates a position where the participant has agreed to follow behaviours voluntarily and can therefore be called to account if they do not. (See Living as your word [S] and Building and eroding [S] trust in chapter eleven, pages 104 respectively 105.) There would also need to be consequences for those who refuse to agree to the agreement, such as exclusion. In circumstances where the person is not voluntarily involved, ensure the rules are discussed so they are understood.

Agreements work well if written down, especially when there are a number of items in the agreement. This makes them easy to refer to and remember. It is useful to have the person sign the agreement. This helps later when using your strategies as you can refer back to the signed agreement. Simple agreements might benefit from a simple verbal agreement such as 'I agree to...'

In most cases, having the agreement made public knowledge (where appropriate) can help support compliance. Having agreed to something publicly creates expectations by others, creates the need within the person to 'live as their word' (see *Living as your word* in chapter eleven, page 104) and makes it more difficult for the person to later deny the agreement.

As discussed in establishing and ensuring consistency, it is very important that the agreement is applied consistently to a whole group. Also, everyone who is upholding the agreement does so to ensure they cannot be played off against each other. Authority figures need to be congruent and live by the same rules. Unfairness is difficult to accept, especially when it represents 'Do as I say, not as I do'.

Agreements should generally include the following (Schoel, Prouty and Radcliffe, 1988 and Typo Station, b undated):

- Respect for self, others and the environment (which includes such things as equipment, buildings and the natural environment).
- Adherence with safety and behaviour guidelines.
- Working towards own goals and group goals (when in group settings).
- Giving and receiving constructive and positive feedback (including speaking up when things are not right and listening to the feedback of others).
- Consequences for failure to comply.

The term feedback is used in this book to indicate communication that is the result of a prior behaviour. It refers to providing information back to the instigator based on how the behaviour affects those around them.

Agreements might also include (Gibbs, 1994):

- Not using putdowns. A putdown is an insult or negative comment used to lower the self esteem of another, e.g., calling someone an idiot. It could be considered a subset of respect rather than having its own point. Because it is so common, it can be useful to mention specifically.
- Listening.
- The right to pass, e.g., not having to respond to specific questions in group meetings.
- Challenge by choice enabling participation to a level of challenge decided by the person, e.g., not completing a rock climbing activity (Priest and Gass, 1997).
- Living as your word, e.g., following through on all agreements (Typo Station, c undated).
- No excluding anyone (Schoel, Prouty and Radcliffe, 1988).

You need to be careful when framing agreements only to include those actions that can legitimately and fairly be asked of people. Respect is something that can be asked of anyone. Respect referred to here is about treating others with consideration. It does not mean honoured, holding in high esteem or liking someone. It is about showing basic respect to others because they are people. Basic respect can include making appropriate eye contact when talking and listening, listening to others, not interrupting, not using putdowns, not spreading rumours and taking care not to damage others' property. Irrespective of the relationships between people, these actions to show respect can be carried out.

There are some concepts that do not always work well in an agreement. This is because it is either deeply embedded in our emotional being rather than our rational thoughts, such as trust, forgiveness and loyalty, or has a dual nature that can easily be confused as in the case of trust. You cannot force one person to trust another, as trust is something that requires the building of a relationship. It comes from more our emotional rather than rational thinking. Imagine if someone came to you and wanted you to agree to trust someone you dislike. Would you? Could you?

The dual nature means you can trust other people such as when making agreements and you are also deemed trustworthy by acting in a trustworthy manner. Asking someone to act in a trustworthy manner is not difficult. So why not exclude trusting others and only include being trustworthy? If trust and trustworthiness become fused together, it can be difficult to explain clearly or make judgement on. It then makes it more complicated and you want the agreement to be easy to understand. Trust has huge potential to support change. However, it is best left out of written agreements and instead used to help enforce the agreement such as, 'You agreed to arrive on time and then continue to be late. Is that building trust?'

Ideas in the strategies section (see Using your agreement [S] in chapter eleven, page 105) will help you get the most out of agreements.

Chapter four
Ways we communicate

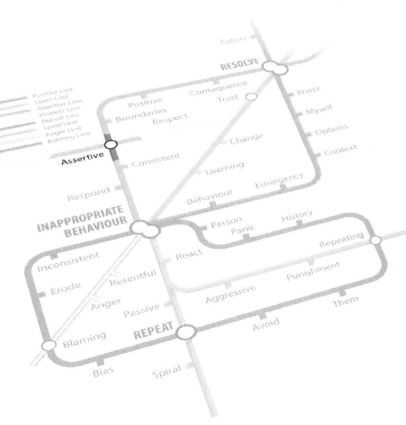

When encouraging appropriate behaviour, understanding the way in which we communicate is critical to gaining successful outcomes. It helps us identify inappropriate behaviour and specific components to address. It allows us to model appropriate ways to communicate our feelings, thoughts and needs.

In this chapter, four communication concepts that provide useful tools are discussed:

1. communication channels
2. three communication styles
3. types of aggression
4. I-messages and You-messages.

These tools will help in assessing what the behaviour of others is communicating, as well as providing strategies for your response.

Communication Channels

Aim	Using word content, tone and body language to understand what elements are contained in the behaviour.
Action	Identify any potentially significant words, tone and body language.

In Practice

When a message is communicated, it consists of the content (what is said), the tone (how it is said) and the body language (the subliminal body expressions displayed when it is said). Content, tone and body language are known as communication channels. All three channels help us communicate our messages. The relative importance of the separate communication channels in any message is word content making up around 30 to 40 percent, with tone and body language combined at 60 to 70 percent (Hickson, Stacks and Moore, 2004).

So, when trying to understand someone's behaviour or develop a response, you should think not only about the content of what is said but also the tone and body language accompanying it.

We do this naturally in everyday conversation so this is nothing new. It is about being conscious of it to make sure you use this to good effect.

Subtle changes in any of these three communication channels can change the meaning substantially, in some cases, to the exact opposite. The words, 'that's OK' can change from meaning yes to meaning it is not OK, by adjusting the tone and/or body language. That makes a difference in how people respond.

This tool can also be used to analyse behaviour in the behaviour step. There are times when there is a mismatch in the message being provided through the different channels. The choice of words might be directly contradicted by the speaker's body language and/or tone of voice. This could be either intentional or unintentional. You can use the information identified from each communication channel to describe the behaviour more fully.

For example if someone says, 'I'll help you out,' it can be intended and understood as being obliging if offered in a light, helpful manner. When the body language conveys disrespect and/or the tone is aggressive or hostile, it can imply a physical threat. Despite the helpful message in the content the other channels send a different message. You are able to provide feedback that it was not what was said that was inappropriate but the tone and body language that was inappropriate.

You can also use specific variations within each communication channel in your strategies and responses to situations. An initial strategy might use mainly the content channel when establishing a boundary by saying 'that's not OK'. The body language and tone could be friendly and helpful. If the issue continues, the same words can be used with a more directive tone and disapproving body language. In this way your response can be significantly altered to suit the situation.

Three communication styles – passive, assertive and aggressive
(Adapted from McKay, Davis, and Fanning 1983; and Typo Station, a)

Aim	To identify the style of communication being used.
Action	Review the communication in all three channels for signs of passive, assertive or aggressive content.

In Practice

A way of assessing the messages being communicated is to view it as having three possible styles: passive, assertive or aggressive. These styles relate not only to the words, tone and body language used but also the demeanour, attitude and intent.

Aggressive communication lacks respect for others' rights as the person tries to influence the situation for their own benefit. There is disregard of the feelings of others using attack and blame, and it can include the use of abuse, putdowns and even physical aggression. Aggressive communication attempts to influence using fear and intimidation to make others feel inferior or threatened. In many cases the messages are specifically directed at someone by using a 'you' statement (see *I-messages* and *You-messages* on page 40 for more information).

The other side to this is passive communication. This occurs when the person does not directly express their feelings, thoughts, needs or wishes. They might avoid making a decision and even pretend not to care. When treating their needs as unimportant or inferior, they exhibit a lack of respect for their own rights in the situation. In some cases they use indirect means to communicate, such as avoiding the person or refusing to talk as a signal that a problem exists. It is important to remember that choosing not to communicate is in itself communicating a message. Passively going along with a group decision is in fact agreeing to the decision. Doing nothing effectively equals agreement.

Between aggressive and passive lies assertive communication. Someone who is assertive tries to find solutions while defending their own rights and the rights of others. This defence of their own rights, however, is not at the expense of others' rights. It is characterised by direct statements regarding their feelings, thoughts, needs and wishes. These statements come in the form of I-messages (see page 40 for more information). They listen to others and actively seek information. And, to develop solutions, they are willing to negotiate.

These three styles can be considered a continuum with aggressive and passive communication being on either side of assertive communication. As with any continuum, the level to which it occurs can vary. For example, aggressive behaviour can range from simple indifference to what someone thinks to threats of or actual violence. A summary of the three types is listed in the diagram.

Three Communication Styles Continuum

Passive	Assertive	Aggressive
• Does not directly express feelings, thoughts, wishes or needs	• Defends own rights while respecting the rights of others	• Lacks respect for others' rights
• Subordinates needs to those of others	• Makes direct statements regarding feelings, thoughts, needs and wishes	• Often disregards the feelings of others
• Lacks respect for own rights	• Listens to others	• Attacks or blames others or humiliates
• Uses indirect means to communicate (e.g., not talking to signify anger about something)	• Communicates using I-messages	• Uses putdowns (abuse)
• Avoids making decision (e.g., pretends not to care – 'you decide')	• Is willing to negotiate	• Communicates using You-messages
	• Attempts to find solutions	• Makes others feel unsafe or threatened
		• Attempts to influence through fear or intimidation

It is important to note that someone can use an aggressive form of expression without exhibiting or intending any threatening or violent behaviour. For example, adopting a whining tone can be a form of disrespect used to mock others. This still would be classified as 'aggressive' despite the absence of threat or violence.

Assertive behaviour tends to be appropriate, including attempting to right a prior wrongdoing. Trying to correct a wrong is a behaviour you would want to encourage. If the behaviour is on the aggressive side of the continuum, then there is a need to take action to ensure the rights of others. Aggressive behaviour (especially physical aggression) needs to be handled appropriately and is discussed further in the emergency step on page 56 and strategies on page 118.

On the passive side of the continuum, the need to take action can be less clear. If a person is passive because of another's aggressive behaviour, addressing the aggression is reasonable, as would supporting the victim to building skills to be assertive.

A person's failure to respect their own rights through passive behaviour is not always caused by the behaviour of others. If a person fails to speak up about how they feel, it could be due to their own decision, rather than not being given the opportunity to say something. Forcing them to voice their opinion can be overriding their right to say nothing. At other times it might be safer physically or emotionally not to inflame the situation. It might achieve a longer-term outcome to accept the use of a passive response. Passive communication is not as clear-cut as aggressive communication.

By asking yourself whether a behaviour and/or communication is passive, assertive or aggressive enables you to begin describing the behaviour. Also to focus on and gather evidence of what just occurred. This provides the first clues towards what strategy is needed.

Types of aggression

Let's now look more closely at what aggression is and how it relates to violence. The following information is meant to serve as background information only to help understand aggression.

Anyone in circumstances where serious aggression/violence is present should seek appropriate help. This book is not intended to provide in-depth support for these types of situations.

Definitions of Aggression and Violence

Anderson and Bushman (2002) in *Human Aggression* provide the following definitions of aggression and violence:

> 'Human aggression is any behavior directed toward another individual that is carried out with the proximate (immediate) intent to cause harm. In addition, the perpetrator must believe that the behavior will harm the target, and that the target is motivated to avoid the behavior ...' (p. 28).

> 'Violence is aggression that has extreme harm as its goal (e.g., death). All violence is aggression, but many instances of aggression are not violent.' (p. 29)

The focus and discussion here will be on aggression, not violence.

Two ways we are aggressive

There are two ways in which aggression is exhibited: overtly and in relationships (Little, Jones, Henrich and Hawley, 2003).

Overt aggression

Overt aggression consists of verbal and physical behaviours directed openly at the target, such as threatening, insulting, name calling, teasing, pushing, kicking, hitting, destroying their property, etc. Researchers found that 'evidence exists showing that boys and men are more physically and verbally aggressive than girls and women', and that the difference starts at an early age and remains similar through all age groups (Fung, Raine and Gao, 2009).

Relationship aggression

Relationship aggression, also known as indirect, relational, or social aggression, is intended to damage friendships, social status or feelings of inclusion. This can be accomplished by the threats of or actual withdrawal of friendship or group acceptance/inclusion, writing nasty notes to others, making them look stupid, spreading rumours, gossiping, attacking their self-esteem, etc. As this can be done secretly, even anonymously, it can make identifying the actual aggressor difficult and the problem harder to resolve.

Various forms of relationship aggression are more often used by girls up to the age of 18. Studies have suggested there is no gender difference in adults exhibiting this kind of behaviour, and in some studies no difference was found between boys and girls, either. This type of aggression is frequently the type shown on television (Coyne, Archer, and Eslea, 2006).

Two reasons why we are aggressive

There are two prime drivers of aggression: reaction and premeditation. They become important when assessing the risk of aggression, which is discussed later in the emergency step (See chapter six, page 57: aggression risk assessment).

Reactive Aggression

Reactive or hostile aggression is 'impulsive, thoughtless (i.e., unplanned), driven by anger, having the ultimate motive of harming the target, and occurring as a reaction to some perceived provocation. It is sometimes called affective, impulsive, or reactive aggression.' (Anderson and Bushman, 2002, p. 29). Because reactive aggression is a term easily grasped, it is the term used in this book.

Fung, Raine, and Gao (2009) further describe reactive aggression as 'involving high emotional arousal, impulsivity, and an inability to regulate or control affect...' (p. 473). Controlling affect refers to being in control of one's moods, feelings or emotions.

Reactive aggression is by far the more common of the two types of aggression. But the fact that it is committed in the heat of the moment in no way excuses, justifies or minimises its gravity.

Premeditated Aggression

Premeditated aggression is a means of obtaining a goal beyond harming the victim. It is done proactively (Anderson and Bushman, 2002). It is also sometimes referred to as instrumental aggression as it is used as a tool or instrument in which to achieve a goal. This is far less common than reactive aggression.

Fung, Raine, and Gao (2009), who refer to this as proactive aggression, describe it as, 'purposeful behavior aimed at gaining a reward or social dominance over others, whereas reactive aggression has been characterized as a response to provocation or a perceived threat...' They go on to state that it 'has also been viewed by others as more pathological and a more serious form of aggression,' (p. 473).

The above information forms the basis for the next tool for assessing aggression.

Aggression types

| Aim | Understand the type of aggression being used. |
| Action | Identify the 'way' they are aggressive and the overarching reason 'why'. |

In Practice

When aggression is identified in the communication, the next step is to determine if it is overt or relationship aggression and whether it is reactive or premeditated. The diagram below illustrates these four possible combinations of aggression.

Aggression types

Reasons why aggressive	Ways of being aggressive	
	Overt	Relationship
Reactive	Reactive overt aggression	Reactive relationship aggression
Premeditated	Premeditated overt aggression	Premeditated relationship aggression

Combining the appropriate 'way' with the 'why' reveals a more in-depth clarification of the behaviour. This provides additional information when using the behaviour, emergency and context steps discussed in chapters five, six and seven, respectively.

I-messages and You-messages – constructing solutions or blaming
(Adapted from Cornelius, Faire and Cornelius (2006); Gibbs, 1994; Lange and Jakubowski, 1976; Luckner and Nadler, 1997)

Aim	Determine whether an assertive I-message or a blaming You-message was used.
Action	Assess the verbal content of the communication.

In Practice

This tool extends the three-communication-styles tool by focusing on the actual words being communicated (content channel). Our language provides many choices of words and ways to construct sentences. Some people are more skilled than others at getting a message across without inflaming a situation. Blaming someone during a discussion makes things harder to resolve because no one likes being blamed.

I-messages

I-messages provide a framework where feedback can be safely offered, as it avoids putdowns, judgement or assigning blame.

There are three types of information when providing effective feedback to someone about inappropriate behaviour. These are: description of the behaviour, the feeling the behaviour creates, and the effect that the behaviour has. A description of the behaviour is necessary to inform the person of the exact nature of the problem. This should always be included in the message. Also including either how it makes you feel or what the effect is will normally be sufficient to communicate the problem effectively.

How the behaviour makes you feel and its effect are related but they are not necessarily one and the same. For example, imagine your friend, Riley, promises to pick you up to go out to a show but does not. Those are the facts, the description of the behaviour itself. The effect, the end result, is that you missed the show. The feeling, however, has emotion attached to it. For example, you might feel angry, resentful, hurt, rejected or a combination of all four. You therefore have three options to communicate this (all of which include describing the actual behaviour):

1. Providing information on all three: behaviour, effect and feeling. In this example, it is Riley forgetting to pick you up (behaviour), missing the show (effect) and upsetting you (feeling). Using this method provides Riley with all the key information about the problem and how it makes you feel.

2. Providing information on behaviour and feeling. Here, this would consist of Riley forgetting to pick you up (behaviour) and upsetting you (feeling). Riley is now aware what the problem behaviour is and that you were upset by it. Riley may correctly conclude the effect was that you missed the show. But not everyone will conclude that. Maybe Riley had such a great time that you being absent went unnoticed. If, for example, you managed to find another way to attend the show, Riley might think you are making too big a deal out of it.

3. Providing information on behaviour and effect. Here, Riley is informed about forgetting to pick you up (behaviour) and your missing the show (effect). This provides all the facts, without an explanation of how you feel. Riley now knows the full extent of the problem, but, after having had a great time, may not understand the depth of the injury, anger or hurt that you feel.

Therefore, omitting any of the three elements carries the risk of not fully communicating the situation. Not only did Riley forget you but Riley doesn't seem to care, either! Forgetful and insensitive! This is possibly because Riley was not given all three elements up front – the description, the effect and the resulting feeling. Communicating all the information might have at least avoided the added hurt of the insensitivity. How we deliver our message can affect the result substantially. This is the where I-messages and You-messages come in.

An I-message states the situation or behaviour and describes the speaker's feelings (option 2 above). The speaker owns their feelings without coming across as judging the person. It promotes a willingness to exchange information, find a solution and to seek a constructive change in the situation. Rarely does this make matters worse.

I-messages are delivered in the form of: 'I feel ... (name the feeling) when ... (describe the situation or behaviour)'. For example, you might say, 'I feel angry when I am expecting a ride and am forgotten.' Using option 1 adds because... to describe the effect: 'I feel angry when I am expecting a ride and am forgotten because I miss the show I really wanted to see.' (Additional examples are provided in the table below.)

You-messages

In You-messages, your messages contain either **you** or **you're** in them. For example, 'You make me so angry because you forgot to give me a ride to the show.' Using You-messages blames the person for the situation and judges them. It can hold others responsible for the feelings of the speaker as well as include a putdown. It invokes feelings in the receiver that can make them defensive or start making excuses. All of this can make the situation worse.

There could be a good reason Riley forgot to pick you up. It might be embarrassing starting with a 'You forgot me' statement only to find out that Riley's mother had a heart attack and Riley rushed to the hospital instead. (Further examples are provided in the table on the facing page.)

	I-messages	You-messages
Example	**I feel** angry **when** people call me names. **I feel** hurt **when** no one asks what I want to do. **I feel** suspicious **when** someone tells me they're doing one thing, then I find out they are doing another.	<u>I feel</u> angry <u>when</u> **you** call me names. <u>I feel</u> hurt <u>when</u> **you** don't ask what I want to do. I get suspicious when **you're** telling me you're doing one thing, then I find out **you're** doing another.
Form	Uses the basic form of **I feel** ... (name the feeling) **when** ... (describe the situation or behaviour). Can add **because**... (describe the effect). Example: **I feel** hurt **when** no one ask what I want to do **because** then I think people don't care about me. Specifically **excludes** the word '**you**' or '**you're**' from the <u>whole</u> sentence, possibly by substituting a more generic term. 'I feel humiliated when you swear at me,' changes to 'I feel humiliated when somebody swears at me'.	Uses the form '**you**' or '**you're**' **Examples of aggressive forms:** *Putdown* - You're dumb! *Blaming* - You were suppose to finish it. *Holding responsible for feelings* - You make me so angry! **Example of passive form:** *Deferring own rights* - I'll just do what ever you decide.
Content	States the speaker's feelings. Enables the speaker to own the feelings. Describes the situation or behaviour that leads to the feelings. Does not judge and helps others to save face. Rarely makes a situation worse. Promotes willingness to change, by providing information on what needs to change. It's a starting point for solutions.	'**You**' immediately blames the person being addressed. Holds others responsible for speaker's own feelings. Blames or judges others; pointing the finger at them. Puts others down. Often makes the situation worse. Invokes feelings in others that can make them feel forced to defend themselves or avoid the situation.
Style	I-messages are assertive.	You-messages are blaming (both passively and aggressively).

An effective I-message does not contain a 'you' reference in it. It is common for those new to I-messages to use the form, **I feel …** **when you** … such as 'I feel upset when you ignore me.' It could be classed as both an I-message and a You-message. However, the 'you' in the statement still blames the other person, making them less likely to cooperate (Luckner and Nadler, 1997). Therefore, the form, **I feel … when you** …, needs to be treated as a You-message and avoided. Everything said prior to the 'you' is generally filtered out or ignored by the person receiving the message.

As soon as they hear the 'you', most people immediately concentrate on looking for what might be an approaching personal attack. It is similar to using 'but' in an argument. This is generally interpreted to mean that you may now disregard everything I have said prior to the 'but'. For example, 'I agree with you, but …' is invariably followed by listing the very reasons you do not agree with them.

In situations where an I-message is appropriate, always avoid resorting to using an ensuing 'you' which can be heard as a personal attack. Instead consciously replace it with a generic term, like 'people', 'someone' or 'anybody'. In most cases you would feel the same way no matter who committed the behaviour, so make it obvious it is not about them personally, but the behaviour. By using a generic term with an I-message, others are more likely to listen to your entire message and willingly change their behaviour. When you don't accuse directly, it enables them to save face and their reaction to you is more open-minded and receptive. It provides an opportunity to start a conversation and work towards a solution.

The simplified version, **I feel … when** … is the best starting point when teaching or learning to use I-messages. It is less complex and gets the most important information out first, i.e., the behaviour and the feeling about the behaviour. The effect of the behaviour can always be added later in the discussion where necessary.

It is worth noting that one can use I-messages negatively in order to manipulate or control someone else's behaviour. For example, 'I feel worthless when we are not together', or 'I feel angry when people go off and talk to somebody else without me.' This use is calculated to manipulate the other person into behaving in the manner the user wants. Another danger in using a template such as this is that it can become predictable or sound false and manufactured. This comes down to what the actual content is and how the message is delivered. To offset this, a number of additional options for I-messages have been provided in Appendix 2.

Analysing Communication

This tool analyses the words used in the communication to identify whether there was a 'you' or a 'you're' in the message. If either is present, then it is likely to be a form of blame in either an aggressive or passive style. This is valuable information. If a person uses an I-message, without any form of the 'you' following it, they are using a positive, assertive means of communication and you may want to consider providing some positive feedback to the user to further encourage this.

Strategic Use

You can also strategically use I-messages yourself. In fact, it is important that you do so. If you are not, then it is possible that you are not communicating assertively and we need to be positive role models [P]. This is also discussed more in the enact step (chapter ten, page 96) when discussing clear communication [P].

There are times when a You-message could be strategically used. When challenging and reprimanding a behaviour that is inappropriate, a You-message can ensure ownership for the behaviour is recognised. This then creates a negative condition or event that hopefully the person will try to avoid in the future.

A You-message can be used in a positive, constructive manner when providing positive feedback to someone. The focus is to reward, recognising them for their personal effort, and assigns ownership of the good behaviour with the person. This serves to reinforce and encourage the good behaviour.

Using I-messages is a great skill to teach others. It allows them to resolve issues effectively for themselves and reduces the need for outside intervention.

Chapter five
Step one: B – Behaviour

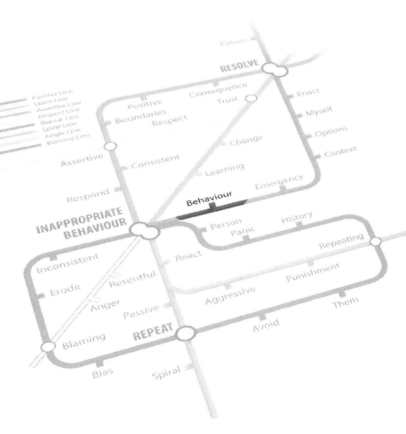

Scenario: Terry

The staff meeting was nearly complete. It was now time to review the progress of the students for any key things to look out for. One staff member begins.

'OK, let's start with Terry.' The staff member shakes her head. 'I'm really not sure what exactly is happening, but Terry is really agitating everyone.' Several heads nod. 'There hasn't been any blatant misbehaviour or breaking of rules that I can point to, but everyone in the group, me included, feels annoyed every time Terry does anything. Is anyone else finding that?' More heads nod. 'I'm concerned that if we don't deal with it, the group will isolate and maybe even start to bully Terry. Does anyone have any thoughts on exactly what it is that Terry is doing that's so irritating?'

'Well, I noticed that when Terry speaks, it sometimes sounds like whining,' another staff member volunteers. 'It seems to happen most when echoing others' comments, it makes it sound like Terry's trying to mock them or something.' More nods of agreement.

B – Behaviour

Aim:	To clearly describe the behaviour.
Action:	Identify the inappropriate behaviour and determine why it is unacceptable.

No matter what the problem, the first step is always the same. The behaviour must be clearly identified before the issue or conflict can be resolved. Unless the behaviour is accurately identified, it cannot be modified. In the example of Terry above, it is evident that unacceptable or inappropriate behaviour is not always black and white or necessarily a clear-cut matter of breaking rules.

Isolating the exact behaviour enables you to communicate more clearly with the offender about how their behaviour is negatively affecting others. From this starting point, you can offer alternatives and encourage them to change their behaviour. Clear identification of the behaviour in question is critical.

How you convey this information is critical as well. It is important to avoid being too vague by using general labels. Telling someone they are annoying is not helpful, as it does not specify what needs to change. There are many ways in which someone can be perceived as annoying, from listening to or playing with a portable device while you're talking to them, being distracting when you are trying to concentrate, showing poor table manners, or being argumentative. To avoid misunderstandings, avoid using labels.

It's also important to separate who they are as a person from the particular behaviour. It does not help a child to tell them that they are bad. They are not bad; their behaviour is bad. You want them to understand that distinction; that it is their current behaviour that is bad, not who they are as a person. This has implications for their attitude as well as their behaviour.

'The problem is the problem; the person is not the problem.' (St Luke's Innovative Resources, 1998). Separating the person from the behaviour conveys a message that it is not difficult to implement positive change. They simply need to change something they are doing, not change who they are or their personality. When defining a person by their behaviour, you reinforce the attitude and therefore the behaviour.

It is 'well known [that] changes in attitude can lead to changes in behavior, but research ... shows that changes in attitude can also follow changes in behavior. According to the theory of cognitive dissonance, the pressure to feel consistent will often lead people to bring their beliefs in line with their behavior', (Plous, 1993 p. 30).

By defining the person by their behaviour (e.g., bad), you reinforce their attitude (I am bad) and therefore the attitude can lead to more bad behaviour. It also works in reverse. If the behaviour is caused by an attitude, you may be able to change the behaviour first which then will lead to a corresponding change in attitude. For example: I am bad but just did a good deed; therefore I am not that bad after all.

There are times, such as the example with Terry, when it is very difficult to define exactly just what the offending behaviour is.

These cases are usually identified by feelings of anger, annoyance or irritation where it is not possible to explain the cause. It is just a feeling. We often then describe it via labels like 'annoying', 'being a pain' and 'acting up'. Finding the behaviour surrounding the label can be difficult but you need to persevere until you succeed.

The person is not able to learn and correct the problem without guidance. Enlist the help of others, if possible, for any insights you may have missed. This is also where a number of principles and tools can help us work out what is going on.

Underlying Principles in Action

Using the scenario with Terry, let's look at what some of the relevant principles can do for us.

- *Unconditional positive regard*: Staff members here are concerned about Terry and the impact on everyone, including Terry, the group and themselves. While recognising the personal, emotional impact on themselves, they focus on trying to locate the behaviour, rather than direct energy towards personally attacking Terry.
- *Being a positive role model*: You might want to ask yourself in this situation whether there are others (including any staff) who are also using mocking behaviour. Has Terry begun this behaviour only after observational learning? Hopefully, no staff members are part of the cause.
- *Responding versus reacting*: Staff members are proactively dealing with the issue. Rather than let it build up and then just reacting to it, they are trying proactively to develop a response that will address the issue thoughtfully and sensitively.
- *Swapping, not stopping*: If the staff are unable to determine the cause, asking 'What change would improve the situation?' can help in the search. Looking at what you would like to see can help clarify the issue. In this case, the possible cause is echoing others' comments in a whining tone. The question is now 'What can we change and/or what can we stop?'

- *Turning problems into skills*: Terry has a communication and/or relationship problem. At this point, the cause has not been identified but it might be Terry just trying to be funny or build friendships through conversation. Some skills for Terry to learn are using an appropriate tone, how to join conversations and friendship-making.
- *Establishing and ensuring consistency*: If there is an underlying culture of mocking communication, it should be readily identifiable. Terry may be the only one in the group who does it poorly and therefore it is causing relationship issues. This overall culture might need to be addressed in order to establish consistency.
- *Providing justification*: The possible social problems that could occur if not addressed justify action.

Tools

The tools relevant to the behaviour step are: agreements, communications channels, communication style, aggression types and I-messages. These tools were discussed in detail in chapters three and four. We will now see how they can be applied using the scenario with Terry.

Agreements

Aim	Clarify what is appropriate versus inappropriate behaviour.
Action	Use agreements to guide behaviour.

In Practice

Agreements help identify behaviour that is unacceptable. Terry's behaviour has more of a general social impact and is about demonstrating respect for others. The mocking creates social tension as others feel they are not being respected.

Communication Channels

Aim	Using word content, tone and body language to understand the behaviour.
Action	Identify significant word choices, tone and body language.

In Practice

Terry's behaviour has been described as having issues in two of the three communication channels – content and tone. The issue is repeating or echoing what others were saying (content) in a whining tone. Evaluating the body language used when the behaviour occurs would also provide further information.

Determining communication style: passive; assertive; aggressive

Aim	To identify the style of communication being used.
Action	Review the communication in all three channels for signs of passive, assertive or aggressive content.

In Practice

At first glance, the behaviour of Terry does not immediately fit with any of the three styles. Only when looking at the less obvious traits does the style become apparent. The reaction of others in the group indicates a lack of respect. Terry might not realise that the actions are disrespectful or that continuing to do so shows a disregard for others' feelings. It could possibly be humiliating or embarrassing for others in the group when it occurs. Therefore, the conclusion is the behaviour has aggressive tendencies.

Aggression type

| Aim | Understand the type of aggression when present. |
| Action | Identify the 'way' they are aggressive and the overarching reason 'why'. |

In Practice

Having established that there are aggressive tendencies, we can now explore the type of aggression shown.

| Reasons why aggressive | Ways of being aggressive | |
	Overt	Relationship
Reactive	Reactive overt aggression	Reactive relationship aggression
Premeditated	Premeditated overt aggression	Premeditated relationship aggression

It is clear that the 'way' is relationship aggression. Terry is likely to be making others look stupid and attacking their self-esteem through the lack of respect being shown. What is less clear is the 'why'. The behaviour occurs in response to others' comments, which could be classed as reactive. But without further investigation it is not possible to discount this not being premeditated relationship aggression. Understanding this further is the task of the context step (chapter seven, page 64) in the BECOME process.

I-messages and You-messages

| Aim | Determine if an assertive I-message or a blaming You-message was used. |
| Action | Assess the verbal communication. |

In Practice

Having no examples of the actual messages Terry uses means this tool cannot be used. It is redundant in this case as we have been able to determine the style is aggressive. This illustrates that all the tools are not relevant depending on the circumstances. In any situation it is about selecting the right tool for the right job.

However, if there were other examples from Terry of communication like, 'You're an idiot. I was only having some fun,' then we could use the tool. The obvious You-message and putdown in this statement indicates an aggressive style.

Chapter six
Step two: E – Emergency assessment

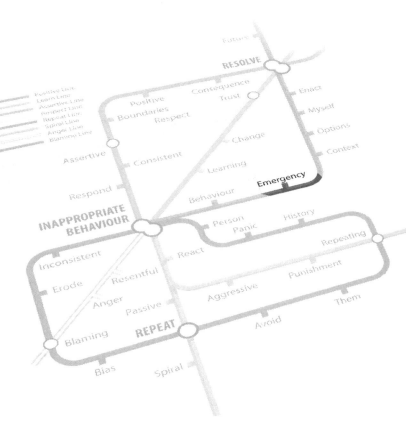

Scenario: Micah and Peyton

The sun is setting as you walk towards the recreation hall. A new group of young participants have been on site for only three hours but you can hear tension in the voices. Outside the hall, amidst the group, Peyton shouts an insult at Micah. Micah is storming away, followed by a staff member Chris. Stopping Micah turns and screams a threat and then charges back up the slope towards the group. Chris stands in the way, firmly commanding Micah to stop. With all the momentum Micah pushes past, knocking Chris to the ground.

You run and intercept Micah before the edge of the group. Again Micah threatens Peyton and the group begins to spread out. Peyton stands smiling and teases Micah again. You try to calm Micah down and keep them separated. Chris quickly arrives and begins to talk to Peyton to stop the continued teasing.

Micah stops shouting and starts to step away as things look to be coming under control. Abruptly, Micah pushes past you and, catching Chris off guard, grabs Peyton. They begin to wrestle. Chris tries to separate them and you hold onto Micah's arms. Peyton by now has lost the earlier bravado. 'Let go, both of you', Chris commands. They both let go and Peyton slowly backs away. With Chris guiding the way, they move out of Micah's sight. Micah is simmering but makes no move to follow Chris and Peyton.

E – Emergency Assessment

Aim	Keep everyone safe.
Action	Determine if there is any danger or risk in the situation.

In Practice
By viewing the situation though a safety lens you are considering the likelihood of danger occurring, any danger that is present, and the possible consequences. You need to consider this in relation to the person enacting the behaviour and others involved including bystanders and, of course, yourself. Is immediate action required to

manage, reduce or eliminate the risk of injury? In the Micah and Peyton scenario, Chris tries to physically intervene and is lucky not to have been hurt.

This requires you to think about other dangers that might not just involve physical safety – things such as emotional safety, the danger of creating a negative norm within a group or that consistency may be compromised. Bullying is a significant issue and it can involve 'psychological, emotional, social or physical harassment', (Field, 1999) so it is important not to focus solely on the physical risk. Bullying is also not just a schoolyard problem, as it also occurs frequently in workplaces.

It is logical to deal with the biggest or most dangerous risk first. But do not let that distract you completely from lesser risks. They can develop into bigger issues with lightning speed if you let them slip while focusing only on the most imminent problem. A simple, quick solution now might avoid a bigger, more complex problem later on. With the Micah and Peyton scenario, things could have been different. If a staff member had been able to stop Peyton continuing the insults as Micah walked away, the final confrontation would likely not have happened.

There are two tools, the aggression risk assessment and response intensity, that help understand the situation.

Tools

Aggression risk assessment

Aim	To assess the possibility of an assault occurring.
Action	Consider the emotional and physical state and past history of the person for risk factors for assault.

In Practice

The most common cause of aggression is some type of interpersonal provocation (Anderson and Bushman, 2002). Whether this is real or imagined, it still has the same effect. Serious aggression or violence rarely occurs without some indicators present in the behaviour leading up to violence foreshadowing it (Mayhew, 2000).

The following 'ESP' risk assessment is based on an assessment model used by the San Francisco Police Academy (undated). There are three categories of risk factors made up of related items. The tool can be summarised as:

Category	Items
E – Emotional arousal	Fear, frustration or intimidation
S – Signs, state and symptoms	Drugs, illness and injury
P – Past history of aggression	Recent or past violent history

E – Emotional arousal

It's important to note that there is nothing wrong with having and expressing emotions, and no emotion should be considered bad in and of itself. It is the behaviour that comes from those emotions that is the problem if inappropriate. As well as the loss of self-control that can also occur when highly aroused.

In the behaviour step you would have gathered useful information to use with the ESP. Having determined the communication was aggressive, the aggression type assessment will help determine if it was reactive or premeditated, and if it was overt or relationship-based. From this starting point, you assess the emotional arousal.

The emotional arousal refers to three key emotional states: fear, frustration and lack of emotion. Each requires a different response. Fear and frustration occur from a reaction to the situation. Those who are fearful will generally move to avoid the conflict. But in situations where they feel conflict is unavoidable, that fear can lead to aggression (Spanovic, Lickel, Denson and Petrovic, 2010). Trapped, they see attack as the only option for defence.

Anger has been linked to aggression as it provides an approach motivation. Angry people generally 'approach the source of the anger with the goal of confronting it', (Spanovic, Lickel, Denson and Petrovic, 2010, p. 2). Frustration is caused by the interference or blocking of a goal. So when looking at the differing behaviour between an angry person and a frustrated one, it can be difficult to distinguish any difference (Arrajj, 2010). When assessing the risk of aggression, there is no real benefit in distinguishing between them

(The San Francisco Police Academy, undated). It may, however, affect the way the issue is handled and resolved.

When aggression is premeditated (intimidation), it is acted out in an unemotional way. There is a lack of empathy and some type of blaming justification. They have some incentive or specific goal they want to achieve and believe they will get away with it and successfully achieve the goal (San Francisco Police Academy, undated).

If fear, frustration or intimidation is present, we can expect the risk to increase with the level of arousal. The San Francisco Police Academy uses three descriptions when rating the risk for fear and frustration. These are, ranked lowest to highest: not present, somewhat present but does not interfere with social interactions, or significantly present and interferes with social interactions. If someone is using intimidation, then you should assume the risk is high.

S – Signs, state and symptoms

Arrajj (2010) discusses the San Francisco Police Academy's method, using signs of drug imbalances, the state of an illness, and symptoms from a brain injury to further understand the risk factors of aggression.

- *Drug (Delirium)*: causes a temporary change in brain chemistry. This can be from intoxication states (alcohol and other drugs), psychoactive drug withdrawal and insulin shock (diabetics experiencing low blood sugar levels). There is a link between substance abuse and violence.
- *Illness (Decompensation)*: periods when a person with a serious mental illness is in a psychotic state. This may be due to the illness worsening, drug taking or not having taken their prescribed medication. There is a link between decompensation and violence, which is more robust with certain diagnoses, e.g., chronic paranoid schizophrenia and bipolar affective disorder.
- *Injury (Dementia)*: the permanent change in a person's brain structure associated with confusion or higher rate of

disruptive and potentially dangerous behaviour. Examples include Alzheimer's disease, AIDS-related dementia, temporal lobe epilepsy, and traumatic brain injuries, such as head injury and heat stroke.

As with emotional arousal, the more risk factors present, and the more severe the presentation, the higher the risk.

P – Past history of violence

One of the best predictors of violence is a person's past history of violence (Mayhew, 2000). While it is important to avoid stereotyping, this does need to be kept in mind. The San Francisco Police Academy training also rates living in a violent home setting is a risk factor similar to actually having committed violence. It rates the risk higher if the violence occurred within the last six months versus prior to that.

Assessing the risk

The use of ESP is to review each category – emotional arousal, signs/state/symptoms, and past history – for the presence of the items discussed above. For each item present in the current situation, the risk of aggression/violence increases. And the more that item interferes with the social interactions of the person, the greater the risk.

While the San Francisco Police Academy model uses a scoring system to assess the risk, here the intention is simply to highlight the key risk factors. The more risk factors present/occurring and the more severe the presentation of those factors, the higher the risk. For example a person exhibiting frustration who is also drunk, suffering a mental illness and has a past history of violence indicates the risk is extremely high.

Assessing the risk of assault is a process that is ongoing. Because situations can change rapidly, such as changes in emotional arousal, it needs to be undertaken as often as necessary.

Scenario Micah and Peyton

Aim	To assess the possibility of an assault occurring.
Action	Consider the emotional and physical state and past history of the person for risk factors for assault.

Aggression Risk Assessment:

Category	Items
E – Emotional arousal	Fear Frustration Intimidation
S – Signs, state and symptoms	Drugs Injury Illness
P – Past history of violence	Recent or past history

Peyton

It is clear that initially Peyton is in control with no significant emotional arousal and is using overt verbal aggression (the insult) but not physical aggression. While mildly intimidating there are no direct threats issued. No other signs or past history is evident. Once Micah closes in physically, a reassessment of the aggression risk is necessary. Peyton is less keen to engage Micah so there was potential for fear to cause an escalation in behaviour. A move away (flight) reaction occurred rather than a moving towards (fight) reaction, and Peyton allowed staff members to take control and provide a way to leave the scene.

Micah

Micah initially is emotionally aroused with less control but not overtly aggressive while walking away. There is an obvious reaction to the situation of frustration and/or anger. No other signs or past history is evident. With Micah showing a reduced level of self-control, there is a high risk of aggression. Micah then becomes physically aggressive, pushing past Chris. As the emotional arousal continues, there is use of further overt physical aggression when wrestling with Peyton.

Summary

Assess the situation for indicators of fear, frustration, or intimidation. Also take care to assess other risk category items (drugs, illness, injury, and past violent history) if potential for them is present. Be mindful of the possibility of an assault occurring if any ESP indicators are present.

Response Intensity Matching

Aim	To ensure an appropriate level of rapport is shown in the response.
Action	Match the level of energy in your response to that of the level of energy and/or danger in the behaviour.

In Practice

The intensity of a response generally should appropriately reflect the danger and/or energy intensity displayed in the behaviour. Changing your intensity to match the situation shows you understand the situation for the other person. At an unconscious level, the actor (perpetrator) thinks that the person responding is similar to them (Luckner and Nadler, 1997). A level of rapport is established because you acknowledge the urgency or importance of the situation.

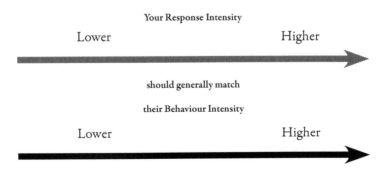

Response intensity diagram

In situations involving physical threat, like in the scenario with Micah and Peyton, a response containing a higher level of urgency and intensity is appropriate. A strong response matches Micah's aggression. Once you are at a similar level, this may enable you to lead the intensity. If you begin to slow or calm down, the other person may follow your lead and do the same (Gilligan, 1987).

If it involves a minor issue and emotions are running high, then a more subdued response from the start is the better option. Playing down the issue by calmly or nonchalantly taking control may stop feeding the behaviour. In this case, you do not 'buy into' the intensity. There are times when not using a matching intensity approach will provide better results.

Chapter seven

Step three: C – Context

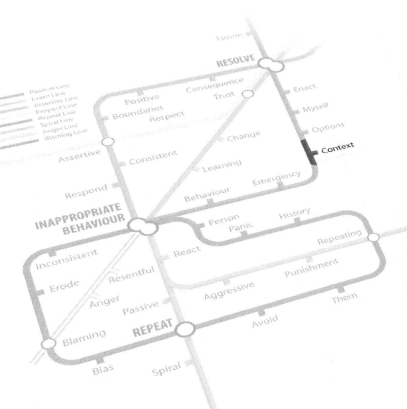

Positive Line
Learn Line
Assertive Line
Respect Line
Repeat Line
Spiral Line
Anger Line
Blaming Line

RESOLVE

Future

Consequence

Positive

Trust

Enact

Boundaries

Myself

Respect

Options

Change

Context

Assertive

Consistent

Learning

Respond

Behaviour

Emergency

INAPPROPRIATE
BEHAVIOUR

Person

History

Panic

Repeating

Inconsistent

React

Erode

Resentful

Punishment

Anger

Passive

Aggressive

Them

Blaming

REPEAT

Avoid

Bias

Spiral

Scenario: Jordon

Everyone is relaxing, enjoying the sunshine. Your group has worked well together. Jordon walks past and asks, 'Where's the bathroom?' Pointed towards it, Jordon moves on, heading past a group of three who begin to talk in low, hushed whispers. Their conversation pauses as Jordon passes. Jordon stops.

'What the hell are you saying about me?' Jordon yells. The group looks at each other and shake their heads. Nothing. Dead silence. 'You're all going to get it', Jordon threatens and storms off towards the bathroom.

C – Context

Aim	Identify any other factors potentially contributing to the situation.
Action	Review the history, circumstances and situational context surrounding the behaviour.

In Practice

Behavioural issues rarely occur without prior events influencing the current behaviour. There can be a history that needs to be uncovered to adequately deal with it. Otherwise you could be dealing only with the reaction and not necessarily the cause. So, assess all the known information relating to the people involved, the history of the situation and the behaviour. You are trying to establish the needs and the triggers. This becomes the context.

While the actor tends to focus on the context, this does not mean they have correctly understood the situation. Assessing their perception of the triggers, therefore, provides a reality check. For us to fully understand the situation from their perspective, we need rapport and empathy. This allows us to understand what need the person is trying to meet.

It is easy to blame an issue on someone's personal failings whereas they will blame it on the situation. Sorting out the difference between these two is the goal of this step. The blaming bias principle below will help us avoid bias either way. By looking for patterns we can look for clues in the relationship between the person and their context.

The context is about seeing the bigger picture.

Principle

Blaming Bias

People have a need to understand and make sense out of their experiences. We make guesses (known as attributions) about the causes of behaviour in others and ourselves. However, we have a number of inherent biases when we make these guesses. Three biases that concern us here are blaming the person, blaming the situation, and blaming the victim. By being aware of the biases, we can guard against making errors of judgement.

- *We blame the person.* (Observer's Fundamental Attribution Error)

When we observe others' behaviour, we tend to overestimate the likelihood that it is due to a personal or internal factor in the person (the actor), rather than being caused by an external cause or pressure. So, 'when we explain another's behaviour, there is a reliable tendency to ascribe the person's behaviour to personality factors', (Reeve, 1992, p. 238).

This is because, from the onlookers' perspective, the external factors might not be obvious. In the scenario involving Jordon, we may immediately feel justified in blaming Jordon because the behaviour is inappropriate and the reaction seemingly excessive. But we lack any history surrounding the incident. Has there been relationship aggression or bullying from the group in the past?

Avoid approaching situations and blaming the behaviour solely on the actor's personality or skills. This fails to recognise any situational factors involved. Both play a part in any given situation. It could be the actor's skills or the situation, but most likely it is a combination.

- *When it happens to us, we blame the situation.* (Actor versus Observer Bias)

While observers tend to attribute inappropriate behaviour to internal (personality) factors of the actor, the actor generally attributes their own behaviour to external factors, like the situation. This explains why a person can have difficulty objectively seeing the part they play in situations. Instead, they focus is on the external factors that triggered them to exhibit the behaviour. Yet, if we find ourselves in the same situation, we instinctively 'change sides' and blame the identical situation on external factors, not ourselves.

This bias protects our self-esteem, but it can limit our understanding and ability to learn and grow through our experiences. For example, Jordon's behaviour might be due to recent or chronic exclusion from the group and therefore a correct perception of the situation. However, the reverse could be true with the exclusion a result of Jordon's inappropriate behaviour. Blaming the situation bias means Jordon is unable to make a connection between acting inappropriately and this creating the difficult situations experienced.

This also has implications on how we, as authority figures, should behave. In order to uphold the consistency principle, we need to be alert to avoid role modelling a double standard. For example, if we observe inappropriate behaviour we might respond saying, 'Don't blame the situation when you're angry; you need to use I-messages'. Then, when the roles switch and we are the ones who are angry and reactive, we claim, 'It's not my fault; it's the situation'. This is due to our instinctive bias to blame the situation. This double standard will undermine consistency and should be avoided. Using assertive communication such as an I-message helps prevent this problem.

- *We blame the victim.* (Defensive attribution)

There is 'a tendency to blame victims for their misfortune, so that one feels less likely to be victimised in a similar way', (Weiten, 1998, p. 648). This is a psychological defense mechanism. There are times when we prefer to feel that people 'get what they deserve'.

You could justify Jordon's behaviour in this scenario on the basis that the group deserved the expression of anger. This could happen, for example, if you have seen the group use relationship aggression, like name calling or exclusion. The problem with this logic of 'deserving it' is that, despite the wrong committed, it does not justify using inappropriate behaviour to deliver the justice.

Two wrongs do not make a right. It rarely addresses the underlying issue and creates the potential for a cycle of retribution to occur. This risks a vigilante culture and undermines establishing positive group norms. While the group in the scenario might deserve being 'brought to justice', it must be done appropriately, irrespective of our underlying feelings.

Think of the tendency to blame the victim as a type of alarm, alerting us to focus on the actor's behaviour as well as focusing on the context. All parties are likely to be contributing to the issue.

Summary

When you feel yourself assessing blame, question yourself as to whether you are blaming the actor, the situation, or the victim. If you are an observer and are blaming the actor, investigate the context. If you are the actor and blame the situation, check that you are being consistent. If you are an observer and are blaming the victim, focus on the actor's behaviour.

Tools

Looking for Patterns

Aim	To understand the context in which the behaviour occurs.
Action	Review the consistency, distinctiveness of the situation and others' actions for possible patterns.

In Practice

Kelley (1967; 1973) suggested there are three important factors in making correct guesses (attributions) about the motives regarding people's behaviour: consistency, distinctiveness and consensus.

Known as the Kelley Covariation Model, it aims to find patterns in behaviour.

- *Consistency* – Is the behaviour the same over time or different occasions? Is the behaviour always occurring? Does it occur at same time of day? With Jordon, you would analyse whether this type of behaviour has happened previously. If you don't already know, you could ask the group, 'What happened there? Does Jordon usually act like that?'
- *Distinctiveness* – Is the behaviour unique to that situation? Does it have the same trigger or a range of triggers? Is the behaviour aimed at a particular entity, group or person rather than a broad range of 'entities'? What stands out about the situation? Does Jordon react that way to everyone or just to this one group? Has Jordon had a falling out with someone in that group? With Jordon having left the scene at this point, you could explore this with others in the group to discern any patterns.
- *Consensus* – Are other people in that situation acting in a similar way? Do others respond to the trigger in the same way? Is it a norm, the way everyone acts? With the Jordon scenario, it would be a matter of looking for other examples of similar behaviour from others within the whole group. If others treat the sub group in a similar way this indicates a broader group issue with the subgroup.

The following table summarises these three factors and suggests examples indicating what various circumstance could indicate. A skills issue involves a personal factor (e.g. learning impulse control) while a situation issue suggests an external trigger (e.g. bullying) that might also need to be addressed.

Looking for patterns

	Looks at	Indicators
Consistency	The behaviour over time	Consistency over time indicates a skills issue
Distinctiveness	Uniqueness of the situation, triggers and entities involved	Regular occurrence to the same situation, trigger or entity might indicate a skills issue or a specific situation issue
Consensus	How others act	Others acting similarly indicates a specific situation issue or a widespread skills issue

Looking for patterns helps overcome the tendency to blame the person by seeing how the situation contributes. It can help indicate when it is not just a situational problem. If someone is repeating inappropriate behaviour, then it points to the need to learn a skill. The scenario with Jordon is inconclusive. Further information is needed to establish whether it is an isolated behaviour, a skills issue or a reaction to a deep, underlying, situational issue.

Looking for patterns helps identify exceptions to behaviours when the behaviour is recurring. These exceptions are defined as: 'the times when the problem is absent or less of a problem. Exceptions include any difference in people's thinking, feeling or behaviour in the past or present ... All problems have exceptions, which give clues to solutions. [It can be more] useful to focus on what people are doing when the problem is absent, or less of a problem, than on what people are doing wrong,' (St Luke's Innovative Resources, 1998).

This forms the basis of the exceptions strategy as discussed in chapter eleven (page 116).

When considering the context, look at the consistency of behaviour over time, the distinctiveness of the context and the consensus – what others are doing. Along with looking for exceptions, this will help uncover any patterns affecting the behaviour.

Perception of the trigger
A trigger, something that acts as a catalyst, can be considered the cause of behaviour. This might be external, such as events or situations the person experiences, or internal, such as thoughts and

feelings. It is anything that has led to an emotional state, need or situation that has contributed to the behaviour.

Aim	Determine if the person understands the context correctly.
Action	Assess if the person correctly or incorrectly assessed the trigger for the behaviour.

In Practice

This assessment is designed to find out if we need to:

1. address the inappropriate behaviour; or
2. address both the inappropriate behaviour and the perception of the trigger.

To do this, we need to understand the person's thoughts about the trigger. There are many instances where an incorrect perception of the trigger leads to inappropriate and unnecessary behavioural reactions. This can be due to automatic thoughts, assumptions and core beliefs (Kassinove and Tafrate, 2002).

Automatic thoughts are spontaneous and fleeting. Jordon might have thought, 'They are talking about me'.

Assumptions are rules or attitudes based on some inference. They generally take the form of 'if-then' rules, or 'should' or 'must' statements (Kassinove and Tafrate, 2002). For example, '**If** I find out they are talking behind my back, **then** I am going to make them pay', 'I **should** always show them who is the strongest' or 'I **must** not let them get away with anything'.

Core beliefs are ideas that people hold about things, people or the world around them, such as 'That group have always had it in for me' or 'Everyone is just looking out for themselves'. This suggests that core beliefs leads to assumptions that subsequently lead to automatic thoughts.

Examining the trigger, we can determine if there were alternative beliefs or explanations. By testing the evidence, an alternative realistic belief or beliefs might be uncovered. This helps us when examining the trigger to determine if it was correctly perceived. It leads to two possibilities:

1. The trigger was correctly perceived.
In our scenario, if the group was discussing Jordon, then the trigger was correctly perceived. That would also depend on what they were saying. The emotional reaction is understandable, even reasonable. But while getting angry is reasonable, the behavioural response was not. Assuming Jordon correctly perceived the trigger, we now know to support Jordon to develop a more appropriate response.

2. The trigger was incorrectly perceived.
Let's now assume the three were discussing a private issue and it had nothing to do with Jordon. Jordon's assumption is then wrong and has incorrectly perceived the trigger. We now need to support Jordon to use more appropriate responses as well as understand the mistake in perception. Reviewing various automatic thoughts, assumptions and beliefs can develop alternatives to help Jordon understand this mistake. Alternatively, the group might need to explain their actions to Jordon. A more appropriate first response from Jordon would have been an I-message such as 'I feel angry when people talk about me behind my back'. The group is far more likely to respond to this by explaining themselves and clarifying what they were discussing.

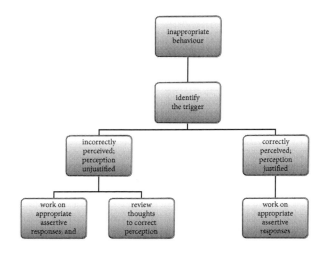

Perception of the Trigger Assessment

Assessing the trigger correctly does not guarantee appropriate behaviour. The issue still can be blown out of proportion, making mountains out of molehills. This would require the emotions and thinking behind it 'to be worked through'. The other extreme is that the person is justified to feel such strong emotions, e.g., being subject to violence. They require support to try and tolerate their emotions to the point where they can deal with the trigger in a more appropriate manner, e.g., not seek revenge. Professional advice and assistance might be necessary.

Summary
The key issue is to identify if the trigger was correctly perceived or not. Do you need to effect a change in behaviour? Or a change in behaviour in addition to the perception of the trigger?

Maslow's Hierarchy of Needs

Aim	Uncover the need the person is trying to fulfil
Action	Analyse the situation to identify the need being expressed through the behaviour.

In Practice

Behaviour is driven by trying to satisfy a need. Maslow (1970) theorised that our needs can be grouped into the following categories: physiological, safety, love and belonging, esteem, and self-actualisation. He also hypothesised that needs are layered, with the more basic (lower) needs having to be met, at least to some degree, before a person would seek to satisfy less basic (higher) needs. For example, someone desperately hungry or thirsty (physiological) would not seek to increase their recognition (esteem) until the physiological (basic) need was met. Although this does not occur in reality in such a black and white fashion, it is a useful general tool to help discern and understand the possible motives of others.

In addition to the above needs, it has been suggested that addiction should be included in this list. This is because addictions can generate physical needs, which are like physiological needs. And where do psychological and psychiatric disorders fit? For our purposes, it can serve us to consider them as separate but very real needs. Therefore, the standard form of Maslow's Hierarchy of Needs has been supplemented with both these extra possibilities.

Adapted Maslow's Hierarchy of Needs

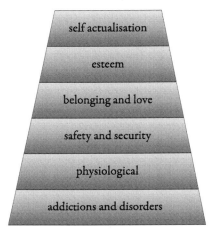

Need	Examples
Self-Actualisation	Realisation of potential, desire to become more of what you wish to be
Esteem	Self-esteem, respect from others, respect for others, achievement, confidence, acceptance and valued by others, receiving recognition
Belonging and love	Family, friendship, intimacy (sexual and non-sexual), social groups
Safety and security	Longer-term safety, including personal security, health, fairness, consistency, predictability, employment, housing
Physiological	Air, food, water, body temperature regulation, sex, sleep, excretion
Addictions and Disorders	Smoking, alcohol, drugs, psychological and psychiatric disorders

Examining the behaviour and context can help identify the need they seek to satisfy. You may be able to support changing the behaviour to a more suitable way to achieve the need. But the need may not be able to be met at all if it is not appropriate.

You should not assume that you have correctly identified the need strictly from your observations. Our scenario with Jordon illustrates this, as a number of different needs might explain the behaviour. Being bullied might affect feelings of safety and security; exclusion from the group might generate a sense of loss of belonging or an attempt to build self-esteem by putting down others. Beware that, when we start making assumptions about a person's need without sufficient investigation, there is a danger that bias will influence us. The information we have about Jordon is insufficient, needing more research and asking more questions.

Psychological and psychiatric disorders are included because some needs are difficult for us to comprehend. It can be difficult to empathise with sufferers of, for example, eating disorders such as bulimia, where a person binges on food and then deliberately vomits it up. Similarly, attention deficit hyperactivity disorder (ADHD) can create difficult behaviour issues that seemingly defy explanation.

Addictions are another area requiring special attention. They can have powerful effects in driving what people will do. While we might immediately think of drug addicts desperately searching for their next fix, it can be more everyday than that. When a young person is caught smoking at school, it might only be treated as rule-breaking. While it is unquestionably rule-breaking, might this behaviour also be driven by addiction? Tobacco is as addictive a drug. The addictive need could trump other needs, such as security (obeying the rules), esteem (getting 'cred' or recognition for rule-breaking) or belonging (peer acceptance). Behaviour can appear simple but, once we begin looking at the need, it can be far more complex.

Finding out what the need is helps us understand the situation better, thereby choosing the right options and strategy. Attempting to address behaviour with a strategy that does not correctly recognise the underlying need is likely to be less effective and at worst totally counterproductive. Some student behavioural issues in the classroom have been linked to being hungry because their families cannot afford breakfast. Supplying breakfast addresses the underlying need not more discipline. Aggressive behaviour might not be caused by the need for esteem from peers but an underlying fear for their own physical safety. Change is unlikely to occur while trying to address their self-esteem and not their safety.

Chapter eight
Step four: O – Options

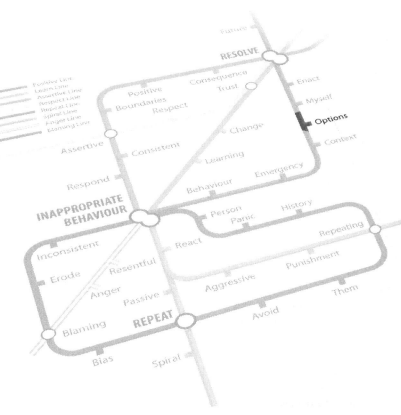

Scenario: Sam and Casey

The days were just starting to settle into a routine: waking up at 7am, and having 15 minutes to get dressed and make beds, before morning chores are allocated. Once the jobs were done, they had breakfast before the day's activities began at 9am. But today had started out a little differently.

Everyone had left the cabin except Sam and Casey. Shannon arrived to encourage them to get up. 'Come on, you'll be late.' Casey lay there and muttered, 'I want a sleep-in.' Sam was lying in the bunk, unresponsive. Shannon tried harder, while Casey outlined all the reasons why it should be a rest day. Neither Sam nor Casey seemed to want to get out of bed. Casey appeared to be the instigator. Shannon moved closer to Sam. 'You're not saying much. Are you OK?'

Sam's face and the darting eyes toward Casey did not go unnoticed by Shannon. 'I'm feeling sick', Sam mumbled, but did not look sick. Something was up. Shannon thought for a moment and then remembered Sam's medical sheet – it mentioned occasional bedwetting. 'OK, Sam, I might take your temperature once lazybones is gone.' Sam brightened and replied, 'I'm feeling a bit better. I really don't want to miss out on anything.' Shannon looked at Casey. 'Come on Casey, up you get'. Casey got out of bed, grumbling, threw on some clothes and left. Shannon smiled at Sam. 'OK, meet you outside.' Now, Sam could have some privacy.

O – Options

Aim	Begin to formulate your response plan.
Action	Review and decide on the most suitable style of response.

In Practice

After assessing the behaviour, emergency and the context, it's time to decide the most appropriate course of action – how best to respond to the behaviour. You must decide on what the main plan is and perhaps even a backup plan. It is helpful to consider a range of options. Be wary of using the same response every time to an issue. It becomes predictable, or worse a habit. Doing things by habit means you do them without really thinking them through.

The response will always involve some type of generalised, high-level approach, such as encouraging or reprimanding. This is referred to as the style. The finer details of how to implement the style are referred to as the strategy. The response style tool provided later in this chapter provides 10 style options. This style then guides the detailed strategy.

First, however, there are some additional principles to consider. These are that everyone has strengths, the power of positive reinforcement, and avoiding using punishment.

Principles

Everyone has strengths

'People have the strengths and capabilities to solve their problems' but concentrating on 'problems tend[s] to blind people from noticing their strengths and solution-finding ability', (St Luke's Innovative Resources, 1998). When emotions are high, it can be hard to remember the good times. But it is important to do so and you should look to see what the person's strengths are – what are they good at? Focusing on these strengths helps see beyond the current problem. Once strengths are identified, you can use them to help resolve the issue.

In the scenario with Sam and Casey, Sam secretly wanted to get up and join in the day's activities but was prevented from doing so by fear and embarrassment. The fact that Sam wanted to get up was a strength, and Shannon used it to help move the situation forward. Once given the clue that Sam needed an 'excuse' to break ranks with Casey, Shannon could use this to change the dynamic of the situation. Casey did not have a fellow conspirator to laze about with anymore. With the bond broken, options that did not work for Casey initially could now work.

Positive Reinforcement

To encourage the behaviour you want, it's beneficial to provide a reward on completion of the required behaviour. The reward should occur during or straight after the behaviour you want. This is known as the Premack Principle, after the psychologist who developed reinforcement theory (McWhirter, McWhirter, McWhirter, McWhirter, 1998; Malott, Whaley and Malott, 1993).

The reward does not have to be anything tangible. Giving a compliment, recognising they completed the behaviour and thanking them can act as sufficient reward. It can be as simple as letting a child do something they enjoy doing after putting away their toys. By matching a positive reward with a behaviour that is less likely to occur, it provides an incentive.

Avoid punishment whenever possible

According to Reeve (1992), 'If there is one conclusion that is firm ... a positive, rewarding approach is more effective than a negative, punishing approach'. This reinforces the positive reinforcement principle. Punishment may be effective at times, and it is unrealistic to think that we can function without it. Given that there are many situations where other alternatives work better, ideally you want to use it as infrequently as possible. Of course, such punishments should not involve being physically aggressive or violent. To help distinguish appropriate and inappropriate or harsh punishment, the term consequence is used. Consequences, signifies providing a reasonable adverse condition as a result of inappropriate behaviour.

There are six reasons why punishment should be avoided (Baldwin and Baldwin, 1998):

1. Punishment often teaches aggression. The use of verbal and physical aggression as punishment teaches by example that aggression is acceptable as a way to respond to situations. Receiving punishment can teach others to be aggressive through observational learning (role models).
2. Punishment causes increased intensity of responses. The emotional and physical response to punishment is greater

than that of other approaches. This increase in intensity creates situations where the person may learn to become increasingly more aggressive.

3. Punishment tends to produce only temporary results. While the behaviour is often suppressed initially, it generally recurs and requires ongoing monitoring and frequent, subsequent punishment. It makes more sense instead to aim for a more permanent solution.

4. People learn to avoid both punishment and the people who punish. Punishment can reinforce skills that help punishment avoidance, like learning to tell better lies. When recipients of punishment begin to avoid the people who punish, punishers then lose the opportunity to control the undesirable behaviour or teach desirable alternatives.

5. Punishment can create wrong, negative emotions. First, it can create negative emotions for the wrong situations. Punishing a young child for running onto the street might instil a fear of traffic (desired emotion) or create fear of the parent (undesirable emotion). Second, if received frequently, it can create general emotional responses such as anxiety, shame, guilt and poor self-worth.

6. Punishment can affect other behaviours as well. If punishment occurs for a variety of different behaviours, people can generalise the punishment as being related to every behaviour. Afraid of doing the wrong thing, they don't do anything and become inhibited, e.g., afraid to speak up, or make a decision because they do not want to be punished for doing something wrong.

In the Sam and Casey scenario, a punishment approach would not have been helpful for Sam. Although keen to be involved, the most pressing need was for Sam to maintain self-esteem and avoid humiliation as a result of the bedwetting. Punishment might have escalated Sam's behaviour, damaged the relationship, established negative emotions and further exacerbated the bedwetting.

Focus on rewarding appropriate behaviour and try to avoid dispensing punishment wherever possible. Use consequences sparingly, only when needed and appropriate to the issue.

Tool

Response Style Curve

Aim	Have a response style that best fits the behaviour and the context.
Action	Choose the style of response to use.

In Practice

The response style curve is a continuum showing a range of 10 possible response styles and indicates which styles tend to be the more positive and supportive. Positive styles are better options, as illustrated by the principles of positive reinforcement and avoiding punishment. The terms to describe the styles are not definitions as such, but guides. They have been constructed to help provide a common language and practical descriptive tool.

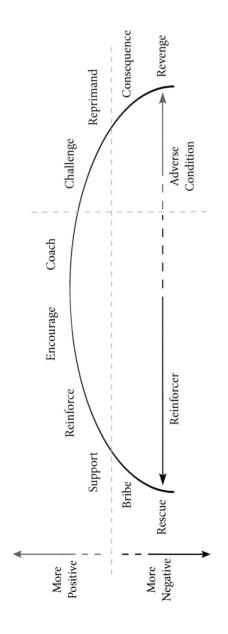

Response style curve

The Style Descriptions

Rescue

Intervening to solve the issue in instances when the persons involved refuse to take responsibility for their behaviour or solving the issue. They are 'rescued' from the situation. Being disrespectful to someone and a friend intervenes to stop it escalating into a fight is an example.

Bribe

This is the blatant use of a highly valued or sought after reward (reinforcer) to obtain the desired behaviour. The bribe is used as a payment for cooperation rather than a reward after completion. The person is motivated solely externally (extrinsically) by obtaining the reward. The expectation of the reward is up front by developing an agreement and it is prominent throughout performing the activity/behaviour (the salience of reward is high). It becomes the only reason for the person to comply. Offering Casey a chocolate bar to get out of bed is an example of the use of a bribe.

Support

Working alongside and providing assistance. By supporting you help the person complete the task. For example, helping clean up a room with them versus their doing it alone, or helping them come up with an appropriate I-message [T] during a dispute. Shannon offering to help Casey and Sam do their chores would be support.

Reinforce

The use of reward or reinforcers to obtain appropriate behaviour, generally once a task is completed. It can be provided without expectation, in which case the individual has exhibited internal (intrinsic) motivation. This is also a means of using the positive reinforcement principle. By completing this task, they can then do something they like. There might be times when the reward is known at the outset but not to the extent that you are bribing them. The reward is not the foremost and only reason to comply. Shannon reminding Casey that once the chores are done they can have a nice breakfast is reinforcing.

Encourage

Reinforcing appropriate behaviours through verbal encouragement. This can occur before, during and/or after the behaviour. Shannon might encourage Casey with 'you did a great job on your chores yesterday. The others really need your help because you're so quick at getting things done'.

Coach

Providing one to one feedback to the person. In a coaching style, you demonstrate required tasks, make suggestions, provide advice, discuss areas of improvement, monitor ongoing progress, promote reflection, and encourage or motivate when performance is not satisfactory. Shannon might coach Casey by asking 'what is different today from other days when you got started with no problems?'

Challenge

Drawing attention to and promoting reflection on inappropriate behaviours without placing your own value judgement or interpretation on the behaviour, e.g., asking, 'Do you think [a behaviour] is fair?' This is without judgement (dependent upon the appropriate tone and body language). Ideally, it is facilitating a discussion where the persons assess the situation and come to their own conclusions. Your interpretation or value judgement may still be provided after their reflection. Shannon could challenge Casey with 'is it fair that everyone else does morning jobs while you lay in bed doing nothing?'

Reprimand

Judging a behaviour to be inappropriate and immediately singling it out as unacceptable. 'That is not OK' or 'That is unfair' are examples of reprimands. A value judgement is placed on the behaviour with the demand that the behaviour must change. Casey might be reprimanded with 'It's not fair to the others that you lay in bed, while they do all the chores!'

Consequence

Providing some type of punishment. It uses a consequence to create a punitive situation (adverse condition) that the person would want to avoid. This should never involve physical aggression, but, instead, could include a range of possibilities such as loss of privileges, doing extra work, or detention. The consequence for Casey might be having to do additional chores, not having breakfast until the chores are done or exclusion for a time period from group activities.

Revenge

Negative action taken not as a means of providing consequences in order to learn, but in retaliation or out of vindictiveness. The adverse condition presented as punishment is emotionally charged and motivated, rather than just a logical consequence of the behaviour. Revenge might be Shannon threatening to make 'life hard' for Casey by getting all the worse chores or 'waking you up at 4am every morning' from now on.

Response Style Curve Discussion

The extremes in response styles are generally neither helpful to the person nor to those dealing with the behaviour. Ideally, maintaining a positive approach means using styles ranging from support to reprimand. That should not preclude the use of the other response styles in some circumstances. As long as you have a plan and good reason as to why you chose a response style, then any option may provide a means to achieve positive behavioural change.

With the scenario involving Casey and Sam, Sam was rescued from the situation of refusing to get up. Once the context was known, it became evident that helping Sam save face would help move the situation forward. The initial approach to both was encouragement or coaching to get out of bed. This did not work. With the ensuing shift in the dynamic, once Sam no longer supported Casey by wanting to remain in bed, revisiting the same styles could then work with Casey.

The response style curve has been based on methods used by behavioural psychologists. Further explanation of the use of reinforcers (rewards) and adverse conditions (consequences/punishment) is provided in Appendix 7, page 152-153.

Chapter nine

Step five: M – Myself

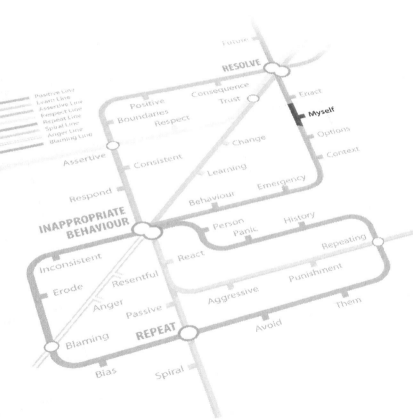

Scenario: Taylor and Bailey

The group was spread out, walking along an old logging track. It had been an easy day, yet emotions were running high. Taylor was walking beside Chris, one of the staff members, about four metres in front of Bailey. Taylor was baiting Bailey as words were tossed back and forth between them. Bailey was known to have difficulty managing anger and Bailey's tone was getting more and more heated. Chris glanced back at Bailey several times, sensing the emotion beginning to rise.

Chris tried a number of strategies to get Taylor to stop fuelling the tension but Taylor continued. Bailey, Chris could see, was about to explode. Clair, another staff member had sensed the tension and drew closer. 'Shut up you idiot,' Chris hissed as Taylor made another wisecrack about Bailey. Bailey stormed towards Taylor, but was intercepted by Clare and Chris. Eventually they calmed Bailey down as Taylor watched on silently.

The rest of the day went relatively smoothly. But there was uneasiness in Taylor's body language and no eye contact with Chris. Chris lay in bed that night reflecting on the day. Telling Taylor to shut up and using a putdown in order to try and defuse the situation was not respectful. Chris made a mental note to chat with Taylor privately the following morning and start off with an apology.

M – Myself

Aim	Having self-awareness of the personal influence you exert.
Action	Assess your part in creating the context and your ability to deliver a positive outcome.

In Practice

It is always important to consider your own part in any behavioural exchange. In many cases you are the independent observer. But there are times when you are totally immersed in the situation, with your actions having a significant effect on the context. In either case, review your part in the context. Even as an independent observer, your role in society can still play a part.

Your cultural background or life experiences can shape what you consider acceptable or unacceptable. Gender role expectations or practices may differ between cultures or because of past role models. Coming from a background where punishment is common can mean less value is placed on other alternative responses. Your job can affect others' reactions, such as a police officer might cause nervousness or distrust in some people because of inappropriate core beliefs.

Each of us has our own world view, biases, likes and dislikes, values and emotions that we bring to any given situation. Many of the principles and tools provided so far attempt to limit these potential influences. They help provide an objective assessment and response. Even with these checks and balances, it is worthwhile reflecting on the factors that affect our judgement and behaviour. By understanding ourselves more fully, we will also help ourselves to understand others. It provides clues on how best to respond to the challenges of others' behaviours.

At times our emotions take over and we react rather than respond to situations. Self-awareness improves our choices in these situations. Reflecting on what we have done in the past helps us to learn and improve.

This step is about self-reflection. The self-awareness checklist provides some questions for you to consider. Remember: everyone makes mistakes.

Principle

Everyone Makes Mistakes

We are imperfect beings living in an imperfect world. It is important to acknowledge that everyone makes mistakes, both you and those you aim to support. To use a film making term, it is a 'miss-take'. We should not be too hard on ourselves if we do make a mistake. Usually we can try again, the next time differently. But we need to ensure that we learn from our mistakes.

An easy way to undermine your ability to support positive change (and therefore your credibility) is not to admit when you have made a mistake. We expect others to own up and take responsibility so it is imperative that we act as role models in this. If you do make a mistake, acknowledge the mistake as soon as possible and apologise sincerely. This ensures consistency and that your actions are congruent, leading by example.

Some worry that doing this will undermine their authority, but not to admit an obvious error shows a lack of self-confidence and leadership. It creates feelings of injustice through the lack of consistency [P] and this strong emotion will erode trust. Acknowledging and apologising enables trust in the relationship to be built or maintained. It is about being fair and showing respect for others. And it demonstrates that mistakes can be addressed assertively.

The scenario with Taylor and Bailey illustrates this. If Chris had not reflected on how the situation was handled, then the issue would not have been realised or addressed. Chris had become part of the context for Taylor. This would have had a major impact on their relationship. Acknowledging the mistake and apologising sincerely helps Taylor move on from the incident.

Tool

Self-Awareness Checklist

Aim	Having self-awareness of the personal influence you create.
Action	Assess your part in creating the context and your ability to deliver a positive outcome.

In Practice

The following questions and ensuing analysis can help with reflection and building self-awareness. They can even form part of a debriefing session or supervised practice. At times some of these questions will be important to address as you plan and/or implement your response. This list is by no means exhaustive and you are encouraged to add any additional review items that you feel are appropriate for your circumstances.

- How have I contributed to this situation?
- Am I at risk dealing with the issue?
- Am I trying to impose my beliefs on the other person?
- Do I have strong feelings about the other person?
- Am I the right person to implement this strategy effectively?
- Do I have sufficient time and energy to devote to this?
- What is the status of our relationship?
- Am I and my message perceived as genuine?

How have I contributed to this situation?
It's important to remain aware of your own impact on the behaviour and address any issues that this creates. With Taylor, it was clear that Chris's behaviour affected the relationship. If you triggered the behaviour, you can still effectively deal with the situation in most cases. Not recognising that you were the trigger will make it more difficult for you to resolve the situation. In highly emotional situations such as a loss of trust, it might be very difficult or impossible to resolve with outside support or help.

Am I at risk dealing with the issue?
Do you have a legal duty to deal with the issue? The person might be a member of the public. What are your organisation's rules and requirements on this issue? Is this an aggressive situation where you are at risk of injury? What are the possible physical, emotional and legal risks? These are important issues to consider.

Am I trying to impose my beliefs on the other person?
Some beliefs are generally accepted societal norms, such as not behaving in an aggressive manner, arriving on time, and respecting others. But others are more personal, relating to taste or preference, such as music choices. If some music is annoying you and it is not your preferred music style you would need to resolve the tension

between your preference and others' rights. Is it fair to impose a restriction due to that preference?

At times separate issues can be confused because of the preference. The issue could in fact be that the music is being played too loudly and is distracting or bothering others. That comes under the realm of a generally accepted norm because it centres on respecting others. However, because of the dislike for the music the issue can become focused on the type of music rather than playing it at the appropriate volume. Reflection can help disentangle the belief or preference from the real issue.

Do I have strong feelings about the other person?

Where strong emotions like anger or resentment are present, it can affect our impartiality and ability to see the situation clearly. Emotions and unresolved issues can build up over time in a long-term relationship to the point where a response is out of proportion to the issue. Frequently dealing with the same issue and/or person might also impact on your perceptions. A minor issue occurring regularly can sometimes become bigger than it warrants.

Have you contributed to the problem by reacting as a result of these feelings? Are you just fed up with the situation? It is understandable to have such feelings and frustrations. However, solving the problem effectively often requires you to appropriately manage those feelings. Discussing issues with those less emotionally involved and therefore more objective can help identify these problems and find solutions.

Am I the right person to implement this strategy effectively?

Sometimes you might not be the right person to resolve a problem. This is not a reflection on your personal competence but what is needed for a successful outcome. Perhaps you are a male and the other person has had previous negative experiences dealing with male authority figures, making them less receptive to what you have to share. Cultural issues may come into play both with gender and acceptance. Sometimes you do not have the 'power' to implement the consequences that you believe are warranted. You may need to obtain help.

Do I have sufficient time and energy to devote to this?
Are you able to deal with the issue right now? Are you able to see it through to the conclusion due to energy or time factors? Being very tired might make you reconsider. To keep a group on track you may need to attend to other things rather than dealing with the issue right now. If you do decide that now is not the time, make sure you address it as soon as you possibly can. Using a delaying statement can do this for you like 'That behaviour is not appropriate and I want to talk to you about why it's not later. I'll catch up with you during lunch to discuss it.'

What is the status of our relationship?
How you deal with issues may differ when they involve someone you have just met versus individuals you have known longer. Having just met, you may feel uneasy raising issues. Or the reverse may be true and you are not prepared to address it because of your friendship. Past problems might cause you to want to avoid dealing with the matter. You might not want to damage a fragile relationship over what may be a rather minor issue.

Am I and my message perceived as genuine?
Can you genuinely implement the required strategy without it appearing contrived? Are you trying to implement a style or strategy so radical or foreign to past interactions that it will not appear credible? Will the strategy arouse suspicion and mistrust by seeming to be contrived? Offering lavish praise for completion of a simple task might be seen as lacking sincerity or that you are being sarcastic. Offering a reward just after delivering a final ultimatum will not be received as genuine.

Always reflect on your part in any situation.

Chapter ten
Step six: E – Enact

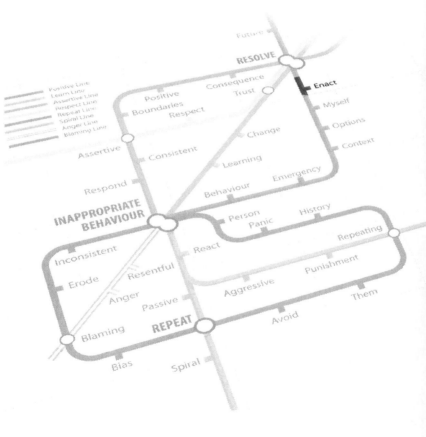

Scenario: Jamie

The last day together had arrived. The first leg of the journey was a two-hour drive to town, where everyone would then board a bus home. Everyone was in high spirits as all the bags where packed into the trailer. As normal all the participants went into one vehicle to be together as a group till the end. A second vehicle with extra staff followed. Time was tight, allowing for just two quick stops on the way. Not long into the drive, the lead vehicle pulled over and the driver got out to talk to the staff in the other vehicle.

'Jamie's not feeling well. All the noise and chatter. Should be OK in a minute.'

Soon after, the lead vehicle pulled over again. 'Jamie's feeling really anxious now,' the driver confessed. 'It's getting worse. The others are singing songs so loud it's hard to think.' 'So should we put Jamie in the staff vehicle instead?' someone asked. 'Umm, I think it should be OK as it is.'

It wasn't long before the lead car pulled over a third time. 'We should have done something before. Jamie's having a full-on panic attack. No way can we put Jamie on that bus. We will get the others to the bus and have to look after Jamie in the staff vehicle.'

E – Enact

Aim	Respond to the behaviour.
Action	Implement your response strategy.

In Practice

All the other steps have helped to gather information and consider the situation. It is now time to put into action your planned response. The scenario with Jamie provides a reminder that not taking action can have consequences as well. Waiting to see if things will get better on their own can sometimes make things worse. Enact is about taking action.

It is during the options step that you decide on the style of response (rescue, bribe, support, reinforce, encourage, coach, challenge, reprimand, consequence or revenge). This broad overview of the response helps guide the use of different strategies. A number of possible strategies for dealing with situations are provided in the strategy chapter that follows. It will provide more ideas on ways to respond to various situations.

Before examining the strategies to use, the enact step examines additional principles and tools. The two principles are providing clear communication and you cannot force change. It then discusses using two tools that helped us previously, the communication channels and I-messages. A final tool, bringing people together to resolve conflict, is also provided to help facilitate solutions to conflict.

Principles

Clear Communication

Whatever style and strategy is used, it is important that a clear, understandable message accompanies it. If the person is unable to understand your message, it will be very difficult to come to a solution. One of the best tools for ensuring clear communication is to use the I-messages [T] referred to in chapter four, page 40).

There are times when you will strategically decide not to use a clear message. This should be a conscious decision with a specific plan to address an issue. 'I am getting pretty annoyed about a few things right now,' is designed to generate reflection on a number of behaviours. The intent is having the persons involved identify their behaviours themselves and ideally rectify them. It is important to ultimately identify the offending behaviour or causes to ensure it is correctly understood.

Communicating clearly is a means of providing a pathway to a solution.

You cannot force change

It is tempting to think that, with all the tools provided, we have the power to change people's behaviour. This is not true. There is no way we can force someone to do something against his or her will in a constructive manner, even when it is in their own best interests. That person has to be ready and willing to make the change. All we can do is encourage the replacement of inappropriate behaviour with appropriate behaviour.

No matter what you do, success or failure does not ultimately rest with you. You can encourage, support and help. That is your role. In the end, you have to respect the right of others to choose their own pathway, irrespective of the obvious consequences. As much as you hope to find an appropriate and effective solution, you can only do your best. Sometimes, you need to accept the things that you cannot change. Knowing you cannot force someone to change helps to put everything in perspective, especially when things do not go well. However, do not use this as an excuse not to try.

Tools

Communication Channels – How You Communicate

Aim	To use word content, tone and body language to support your strategy.
Action	Selecting your words, tone and body language.

In Practice

Communication channels are discussed in chapter four (page 31) and used to help understand how others communicate. The use of word content, body language and tone are important aspects in your communicated response. Strategies can be modified by effectively using the three channels to your advantage.

A reprimand can be communicated in various ways. You might coax, 'Come on, clean that up,' using a joking tone before adopting a sterner one if no action is taken. Or the reprimand might not even be verbal; instead you use body language to signal disapproval. Your strategies can be modified by using different channels in numerous ways.

I-messages

Aim	To communicate assertively.
Action	Use I-messages as the basis of any word content.

I-messages are discussed in chapter four (page 40) and used to help understand how others are communicating. Role model the use of I-messages in your own communication. This will ensure that your word content is assertive and not passive or aggressive. Also refer to the Appendix 2 (page 141) where additional options for I-messages are provided.

Bringing People Together to Resolve Conflict

Aim	To develop a formal agreement as to how a conflict will be resolved.
Action	Use the formal conflict resolution steps when appropriate.

In Practice

There are times when you need to bring people who are in conflict together to resolve the issue. The following process describes how to mediate an issue between two people. 'Conflict resolution involves meeting the needs of two parties in conflict. It's a process of embracing difference, exploring the details, expressing emotions, exploring options and negotiating agreements,' (Typo Station, a).

Generally this process is used for ongoing conflict or when a major incident occurs. Establishing a formal resolution such as this for minor matters trivialises the process, as well as taking up too much time. Therefore, use your judgement on when to use this process. When you are going to mediate an issue, plan out how best to accomplish this.

Things to remember
Conflict resolution involves:

- Describing actions.
- Describing feelings relating to the described actions.
- Everyone recognising the mutual problem.
- Appreciating that this is not a win/lose situation or a compromise in which someone's needs are not met.
- Avoiding the power play, which might win the outcome but in the process will lose the relationship.
- Not using intimidation, which will destroy trust.
- Completion in an emotionally and physically safe environment.
- Promoting a future focus for actions and moving on, rather than the attribution of blame.
- Awareness that it will not work if significant fear exists, if there is a significant history of abuse, or if one or both parties do not wish to be involved.
- Not focusing on getting people to say they're sorry, although they can do so. It is about developing a common understanding of how actions affect the parties.

(Adapted from Gibbs, 1994; Johnson and Johnson, 1994; McKay, Davis and Fanning, 1983)

Ground Rules
The ground rules need to be agreed upon by all parties, by confirming: 'I agree not to interrupt, not to call names, and to work to solve the conflict,' (Gibbs, 1994, p. 119).

Process (Gibbs, 1994)
1. Find a comfortable, private and safe space to conduct the process.
2. Explain the process to the participants individually before starting.
3. Have each party agree to ground rules.

4. Have person A tell A's side of the story using I-messages, stating what happened, how they felt and what they want in the future.
5. Person B restates what A has said the problem is for them, using A's language. Suggested starting statement for B when restating the problem is, 'So, the problem for you is...'
6. Repeat steps 4 and 5 with roles reversed: B states B's side of the story and A restates it.
7. Both A and B then suggest possible solutions.
8. Both A and B work to agree on solutions that are:
   - specific (actual actions named)
   - balanced (both people have actions to take and responsibility for making it work)
   - realistic (will actually address the issues and work to solve the problem).
9. Set a time frame to check in with both parties on the progress of the solutions.

Mediator's role (Typo Station, a)
The mediator needs to attend to the following:
- facilitate the resolution process steps
- arrange the space so all parties sit equidistant (e.g., triangle/circle) and at the same level (so no one towers over another in a potentially intimidating way)
- monitor the process for respectful conversation, intimidation and take steps to maintain the integrity of the process
- stop interruptions
- prompt individuals for their stories and solutions
- ensure solutions (agreements) are written down for future reference.

Responses for interruptions (Typo Station, a)
Should someone attempt to interrupt while it is the other person's turn, you should intervene to allow the speaker to continue uninterrupted. Below are listed some suggested interventions. They provide different levels of intervention depending on the level and regularity of the interruptions.

1. Hold a hand up to the person who is interrupting.
   Continue, facing the person whose turn it is to talk and say, 'Yes, go on.'
2. 'Hold on a minute, A', turn to B and say, 'We did agree not to interrupt, is that not so?'
3. 'B, you will get your say soon; so please be patient.'
4. If interruptions continue, stop the mediation and revisit later.

Chapter eleven
Strategies to support change

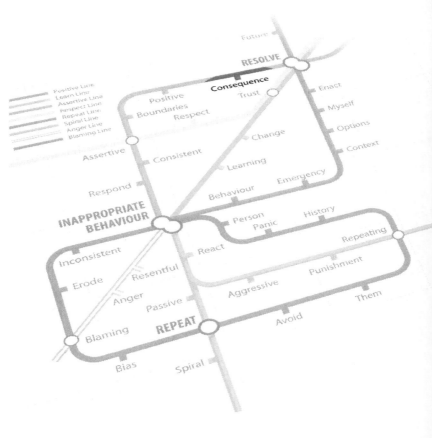

Introduction

What is a strategy? Reber (1995) defines it as 'a plan of conduct or action, a consciously arrived at set of operations for solving some problem or achieving some goal,' (p. 760). As discussed in the options section, strategies are the next level down from the response style. Chapter one outlined the differences of principles, tools and strategies. Principles and tools are used to assess and understand the situation. They gain information. Strategies help support change by being the response. This is a general framework within which to work. However, the real world is never as clear-cut as we would like.

Three tools, the I-messages [T], communications channels [T] and the response style curve [T], blur between tools and strategies. Using an I-message can be both a strategy you use and a good tool for examining communication style. Communications channels and the response style curve can help assess and describe behaviour as well as be used in strategies.

A response style from the curve forms part of a strategy, but it does not give specifics on how it will occur. For example, challenging can occur by naming it: 'Hey, when people do that, it is disrespectful', or by using an I-message like, 'Hey, I feel disrespected when people do that sort of thing'. The response style curve narrows down the broad range of responses, which helps in the selection of possible strategies.

This book is about providing practical solutions. The framework and definitions try to reflect our complex and imperfect world. Attempting to provide a perfect system will distract us from the most important task – supporting change to occur. So this framework attempts to logically explain the process, despite its imperfections.

What follows is an explanation of a number of possible strategies to use.

Naming it

Sometimes people are simply not aware of their actual behaviour. It is a habit. Naming the behaviour brings it to a conscious level where it can be evaluated. Stating, 'Calling someone [derogatory term] is disrespectful', or 'What I am seeing is people being bullied', provides constructive feedback. Naming it can use the adverse condition (like the above examples) and the positive reinforcement (e.g. 'That type of behaviour helps show respect.') sides of the response style curve [T]. It is an effective strategy that works closely in conjunction with I-messages [T].

Some useful terms (adapted from Typo Station, a) when naming, and examples of their application, are:

Choosing	That is **choosing** to be disrespectful.
Going too far	The first time was funny; now it's **going too far.**
Fuelling conflict	Continuing to put someone down is **fuelling the conflict.**
Not OK	Pushing others is **not OK.**
Disrespectful	I find people not listening while I am speaking **disrespectful.**
Eroding (see also the eroding strategy below)	Not doing what was agreed upon is **eroding** trust.

Living as Your Word

The *Living as Your Word strategy* (Typo Station, c) was mentioned previously in chapter three on establishing agreements. This strategy can be used when an agreement is not followed. The person is challenged or reprimanded for not living as their word. This challenge is asking them to be consistent between what they say to people and what they actually do.

It can be seen as their having lied about agreeing to do something. But beware. Calling someone a liar is a very strong statement and will do little to solve the problem because of the negative emotions it creates. Doing so is just likely to damage the relationship. It can also be difficult to effectively link the behaviour to an actual lie. Was it a mistake made during the heat of the moment or a premeditated act? For example, you establish an agreement to stop swearing, and, later, during an argument, they swear. You cannot actually 'prove' they intentionally lied when forming the original agreement.

Call attention to the agreement that they need to try to stop swearing. 'We had an agreement to stop swearing. You need to try and follow through on your word.' Living as your word is subtle. In more difficult cases, a discussion about lying might be appropriate with explanations of the possible consequences. This should only be when blatant lying is evident, such as saying they were at a friend's house when in fact they were at a party.

A similar strategy is to discuss trust. If you do not live as your word, then how are people going to trust what you say? Using the trust theme can avoid the possibility of being drawn into an argument: 'Are you calling me a liar?' You can focus on facts – 'You said X, but you did Y'. You can then link this to the building and eroding [S] strategy. Being consistent [P] might be another concept that could be used.

Building and Eroding

The building and eroding strategy (Typo Station, a) uses the premise that every behaviour will either build or erode the expectations and beliefs of others. Does this behaviour gain or build trust or does it reduce or erode the level of trust? Saying one thing and doing another erodes trust. Following through on an agreement builds trust. To help encourage further reflection, you can use this in conjunction with questioning what is going on [S]. 'Do you think that [certain behaviour] builds or erodes trust?'

This can be used for various concepts such as trust, respect, friendship, rapport, fairness or responsibility. For best results, a discussion about the meaning of the concept should take place before it is used. By first gaining agreement [T] that building is better then eroding, they understand the benefit. Once the goal is agreed upon, coaching, challenging, etc., can be used to identify examples of building and eroding. This works with either the positive reinforcement or adverse condition parts of the response style curve [T].

The building and eroding strategy works best when longer-term interaction occurs rather than a single instance.

Using your agreement

As discussed in chapter three, having an agreement [T] in place is a powerful way of establishing an atmosphere where everyone knows what is expected. Below are some additional strategies based on how you might use that agreement.

Respect for self, others and the environment

Being assertive is about having respect for yourself as well as others. You can draw attention to the agreement to maintain self-respect when individuals are acting passively, and the agreement to respect others when individuals are behaving aggressively (see passive, assertive and aggressive [T] page 33). Respecting the environment includes such things as equipment, buildings and the natural environment. Examples include: littering (not showing respect for the environment), cleaning up after themselves (respect for both others and the environment) and looking after equipment, especially when it does not belong to them (respecting the environment as well as others who may want to use it at a future date).

Follow safety and behaviour guidelines

Being and acting safe is an important requirement. So, listening and following safety guidelines are very important. You can empower others by asking them to help enforce guidelines or to speak up if they have concerns. Accepting the agreement also allows for others to remind individuals if they forget (Schoel, Prouty and Radcliffe, 1988).

Clear directions need to be given at the outset, along with reminders at important points. It can be worthwhile prior to an activity that has risks associated to review the safety and behaviour guidelines rather than letting issues occur prior to intervening.

Work towards your own and team goals

Most people are happy to work towards their own goals. But in society it is rare that we are in a context where we are alone. Therefore, we need to also be aware of and work towards the goals of the group(s) we are in. In many instances there are strong links between teamwork-oriented skills and showing respect included in the agreement [T].

A number of ways to address issues are: 'The team agreed that its goals are [goals], and that actions, like [action], are disruptive and preventing these from being reached', or 'The lack of respect for others is not helping us reach the team's goals that we all agreed on'. Schoel, Prouty and Radcliffe (1988) also suggest using metaphors such as family (where appropriate) and sports teams.

Give and receive constructive and positive feedback.

Ensuring the agreement makes a reference to providing feedback gives permission to provide that feedback. It also contains an obligation by the parties to listen to (receive) feedback and take action to change their behaviour based on that feedback when appropriate. 'I don't care what you say' can be countered with, 'Well, we all agreed that we would receive feedback'. It can then be used with other strategies such as 'respecting others by receiving and taking on board feedback' and 'not living as your word' [S].

The framing of feedback that requires behaviour change should be termed *constructive*. This helps the recipient view it in a positive frame. It focuses on helping them improve. Using the term 'negative feedback' is more likely to be taken as a personal attack and has blaming or other negative overtones.

In situations of passivity, the agreement places an obligation to provide feedback. 'Speaking up when things are not right' allows them to respect their own rights and provides a way to achieve them. The best mechanism for feedback is the use of I-messages [T] and this skill should be taught and modelled.

A key component of receiving feedback is to change behaviour. It is not just a commitment to simply listen and then do nothing. There is an obligation to take action based on the feedback where it is justified. However, there will be occasions where feedback is unjustified or inappropriate. Not doing something about the feedback is reasonable in these circumstances.

When the feedback is inappropriate, some action to acknowledge and address the matter should occur. 'Thanks for the feedback, but the way I see the situation is [viewpoint] and so I don't believe there is any need for me to change' might be all that is needed. Respect for the provider of the feedback needs to be maintained otherwise the process loses legitimacy. This can lead to people opting for less appropriate means of providing feedback. Just ignoring feedback would not be showing respect, but sometimes it can be the wisest course.

Failure to comply consequences

Reminders of consequences can help motivate and keep people on track. As discussed in the positive reinforcement principle, it is far better to take a positive approach. Consequences in an agreement can be a preventative strategy by using them in a reminder. Reactive approaches should be a last resort.

Stopping someone prior to their possibly committing an act with major consequences can act as a circuit breaker on the behaviour now and in the future. It also shows the relationship is a fair and caring one, by demonstrating you do not want them to suffer consequences unnecessarily. But care needs to be taken to avoid repeatedly rescuing the person. At times suffering the consequences is the only way that someone learns from the situation.

Not using putdowns

Putdowns are insults designed to degrade or offend (Gibbs 1994). This links with showing respect for others and, depending on the circumstances, might be such a common form of disrespect that it justifies separate mention in the agreement. It would continue to be justified on respect grounds and therefore could be used together. 'We agree never to use putdowns when talking to or about someone, as it does not show respect for others.'

Listening

The ability to listen may be a skill that is lacking and requires specific attention. It may also be needed to support receiving feedback, so there is a clear understanding of the need to listen to feedback.

Right to pass

The right to pass (Gibbs, 1994) or abstain is an important provision. There are times when not having to participate, for example responding to questions during group meetings, is appropriate.

Challenge by choice

There are times when you will need or want to offer people the choice as to how they participate (Priest and Gass, 1997). This is natural given that everyone has different preferences, likes, dislikes, abilities and tolerance for risks and situations. When and how choice is provided needs to be carefully assessed, as it can undermine the ability to achieve goals if unlimited choice is provided. If a choice is given to the group, a group may collectively conspire not to choose the challenge. For example, if choice is given on providing feedback and someone in a group is not doing their share, the group might decide not to give feedback and the situation will not be resolved. Unlimited choice is therefore not always possible.

Referral to the agreement to provide feedback could break the above deadlock in the example above. 'Things are not going smoothly but no one is saying anything. We all agreed to give each other feedback so now seems like a time when we need to give some feedback to solve this.'

There are ways of dealing with this choice issue. In the feedback example above, a choice might be provided on how the feedback is given. This could be to the whole group, in smaller subgroups, or be in written form rather than verbal. In other cases, you might give the ability to choose on some but not all activities posed. If the group is going on a canoe trip, it is not possible to offer choice concerning every aspect of the trip. They are all going to have to canoe and they are going to have to paddle. But some may choose to walk around rapids rather than paddling them. It is about being mindful that everyone will be challenged at different levels, and allowances need to be made for this.

Challenge by choice does not have to be in the agreement. If there is significant resistance by one person on a particular issue, you might opt to let them have their way on that one issue. There could be a personal history behind the resistance of which you are unaware. A near drowning experience might create resistance to paddling a rapid for fear of capsizing and having to swim. Just be mindful of the impacts this can have on the person and others in a group. If it becomes a trend with the one person, referral to other parts of the agreement might be used to encourage or insist they contribute. 'We agreed to work towards that personal goal of giving things a go. Here's an opportunity to work on that goal.'

Swapping

Swapping the behaviour is a good strategy to employ when a reaction was inappropriate but the reason behind the inappropriate reaction is justifiable. By replacing the inappropriate behaviour with something appropriate, it will enable the need to be met. Swapping to an alternate behaviour that assertively communicates will increase the skills and ability in the future. The situation is a learning opportunity to develop the skills to effectively interact and express needs.

For example, Kate is not looking where she is going and collides into Molly. Molly's reaction is to call Kate names. It is understandable that Molly is upset but using putdowns is not an appropriate solution. By swapping the aggressive putdowns with an assertive I-message, Molly can still express her need, but in a more respectful way.

Shaping

Shaping is using small-steps and intermediate behaviours to shape the behaviour progressively, in order to reach the desired final behaviour (Malott, Whaley and Malott, 1993). Rather than aiming for complete change at the outset, this breaks the behaviour down into more achievable and manageable steps. Each intermediate step is achieved by positively reinforcing appropriate behaviour and using adverse conditions when inappropriate behaviour occurs. This continues until the desired behaviour is reached.

For example, the behaviour goal is for Shannon to stop using foul language. There is one particular word used frequently that is worse than the others. Forming an agreement [T] with Shannon to stop saying that particular target word and maybe swapping [T] it with an inoffensive word like 'what!', is the first step. Now, when Shannon uses the target word, the response is coaching, issuing a challenge or reprimanding, creating an adverse condition. The next time, Shannon might use the forbidden word but remember immediately and add, 'Sorry, I meant to say [alternative word]'. By also using encouragement when the replacement word is used, you help reinforce the use of the replacement word.

After some time, the habit forms and Shannon has begun to use the replacement word consistently and the use of the target word stops. Now that Shannon has dealt with word number one, it is time to work on word number two. Being able to just concentrate on one word is far easier for Shannon than having to remember to stop every swear (cuss) word. It is manageable and you can give specific feedback at the end of a day. 'You didn't say "that word" once today. That's very good!' It is difficult to give specific feedback when trying to stop five words at once and they continue to use two of them. Are they getting better or just using those two words as replacements for the other three?

This process of shaping is depicted in the following diagram.

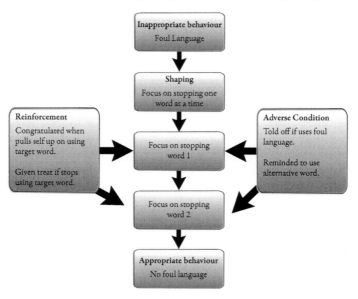

Shaping Strategy

Emotions Are OK

This is an acknowledgment of emotions and that they are valid. You point out that it is not the actual emotions that are the problem but the behaviour in response to the emotions. Anger is a common emotion and it is important to reassure people that anger in itself is not bad and serves a valuable purpose. Anger lets us know when something is wrong and gives us energy to do something about it. But anger creates problems because people do inappropriate and aggressive things when reacting.

'It's OK to be angry, but being angry does not give people the right to behave aggressively towards others'. This strategy is about ensuring that, whatever response style on the curve you use, it is clear that the person's emotion is OK and the feedback concerns the form of reaction they used, which was not OK.

Cooling Off

There are times when emotions run high and it is not appropriate to deal with a situation at the time it occurs. The person or persons might be uncooperative. A simple statement saying the incident needs to be discussed but it will occur at a later time is sufficient. It is very important to ensure a time frame is provided as to when the discussion will occur. 'I'll give you 30 minutes to cool off and then we will talk about it', or 'We will take a break for two minutes, and then I'll check in with you to see if you're ready to discuss the matter'.

This is a circuit breaker and also works the same for you when your emotions might overtake your good judgement. 'I am so angry at the moment I need to cool off. We will talk about this later.' Keep this strategy in mind during the 'myself' step and use it when necessary.

Once the time period is set, keep your word and honour it, even if it is then decided to allow an additional cooling off period. Longer time frames can also be appropriate depending on the present demands of the situation. It might mean discussing the matter after lunch or during the next break.

Be wary of allowing too much time to cool off. Things can fester and another incident might occur before you deal with the first one. Those involved could also return and not want to deal with it, saying, 'I'm over it now, so let's not worry about it.' This will undermine the ability to resolve the issue. When this occurs, insist on following through to a resolution just as you normally would. You can use a statement like, 'Well, you might have moved on, but I have not and want to ...'

Humour

The use of humour can be a subtle means of delivering messages that can bring about behaviour change. It can defuse tense situations. It can be used to develop rapport. Making light of a situation can let a person know that they have done wrong without the need to become too serious, especially when that person is in a heightened emotional state.

Sarcasm is the use of witty language to convey insults, derision or irony. It is a form of humour that the recipient can easily misunderstand and can also become a negative group norm. It is advisable not to use sarcasm at any time. Humour should also not be overused, as this can send mixed messages and confuse people as to when you are serious and when you are not.

Timing

Consider the timing of your intervention (also see cooling off [S], above). In some cases you may wish to intervene before the behaviour is attempted, perhaps by suggesting a good course of action. For example, seeing the person is very angry, you might suggest, 'If you think that's unfair and it's making you angry, then tell them so, using an I-message'. Be aware this might be rescuing them if it is done too often. However, if the choices are between a physical assault occurring or having to rescue, perhaps allowing consequences to unfold can wait for another day.

Other times, you might allow the behaviour to occur normally before becoming involved so that the consequences start to become evident. It does not mean letting it go to its full conclusion but doing 'edgework' (Luckner and Nadler, 1997). This involves intervening during the doing, in the moments before completion.

At this point in time, you examine what is occurring, highlighting any positives and things stopping success.

Owning The Behaviour

Everyone is responsible for their behaviour and must take ownership of the things that they do. It is no one else's fault as to how they react or respond to situations, because they have control of what they do. It is the individual's responsibility as to how they act. For younger children breaking down the word responsibility into its parts helps understanding. Response and ability means their ability to respond. Be clear that while any arguments or excuses as to why they did something can be acknowledged and even empathised with, they cannot be used to justify inappropriate behaviour.

When someone is trying to avoid taking responsibility for a behaviour, some responses to consider include, 'Hang on. The fact that someone does something wrong does not mean it is then OK to [action]'. When they blame someone else a humorous approach is: 'Wow, they just took control of your mind and made you do it?' (Be sure to avoid sarcasm in the delivery.) Irrespective of the provocation, it requires taking responsibility for how they acted. A response is justified but an inappropriate response is not.

Modelling

Using some behaviours may first require a person to learn and develop a new skill. If you are going to teach a new skill, it is important to provide an active demonstration of what is required. Show them what it is about and how to use it. Modelling allows for observational learning.

Use examples of others in the group modelling the behaviour to serve as role models. Of course this only works for behaviours you want to reinforce and encourage; you should avoid modelling inappropriate behaviour.

Coaching

When teaching new skills, not only do you need to model and show the skill, but it is also important to provide ongoing coaching. Do not expect anyone to be able to learn a new skill immediately and implement it correctly without trial and practice. Explain this to the person to avoid the risk of their giving up because they are afraid to fail. Frame the learning process. 'I know it's hard to change things but we shouldn't call each other names when we're frustrated. This takes practice. I can help you out and coach you using I-messages. Would that be OK?'

Getting agreement to act as the coach for the skill and to provide feedback helps develop a collaborative relationship. And it establishes a goal. This will enable improved use of the skill, evaluation of the person's progress and opportunities to offer suggestions on how to improve. Everyone needs to find their own style in using skills. The coaching strategy allows this to develop while ensuring the basic outcome is not compromised.

Logical Consequences

'Setting up a system of logical consequences not only encourages ... responsibility for their behaviour but can greatly reduce the amount of arguing that goes on ...' (McWhirter, et al., 1998, p. 269)

As discussed in establishing an agreement [T], there should be consequences in some circumstances. The consequences need to be real, realistic, justifiable and defined. You need to be also willing and able to carry out the consequences. 'We will send you home' is not effective if the only way home at the time is by helicopter, assuming one is unavailable to you.

There can be situations that are not covered by the agreement but require specific attention for an individual. A specific agreement for the individual will overcome this. You may wish to have the person decide what the consequences will be. 'If I do not stop swearing, I will not get to rent some movies.'

If the consequence is logical, then it is likely to reinforce appropriate behaviour. Coming home late from a friend's house suggests the consequence should have something to do with visiting friends. It might be not being allowed to go visiting for a period of time or a reduced visiting time. Having to complete more chores is not a 'natural' consequence that is directly related to the issue. Some might happily do more chores if it means they get away with staying out later. Not completing your assigned task means you cannot move on to the more interesting activity, which is a natural consequence. This is from the reprimand side of the response style curve [T].

Questioning – What Is Going On?

Similar to naming [S], questioning the behaviour asks the person to evaluate and name the behaviour. Questions like 'What is happening here?' or 'How do you think other people will interpret what you are doing?' place the responsibility on the person to think about their behaviour. They own the evaluation, having determined it.

It also helps you to understand the language being used by the person to describe situations. What you may consider to be a put down, they might describe as simply speaking the truth. 'Well, it's true, he is a ...' tells you more about what the person is thinking.

Questioning has the benefit of not making any value judgement yourself. It is useful when you did not see what happened or are unsure of the identify of the instigator. Turning up on the scene, this becomes an instant version of conflict resolution (see bringing people together [T], page 98). Each person must then provide their version of the event. Because of its neutrality, it offers the use of either side of the response style curve [T] once more details are known.

Exceptions

On occasion, people can feel powerless to change. The problem they're experiencing is so all-consuming that it is all they can focus on. This is discussed in chapter eight (page 78) in the principle that everyone possesses strengths. It is important to recognise when the problem does not occur. The strategy is to positively reinforce times when they avoid the problem, the exceptions to the rule. 'I noticed you stopped yourself from swearing that time, well done.' This will encourage use of the behaviour used during the exception.

Another option is to help the person reflect on the exceptions to understand what they it is that they do successfully. 'Using that swear word is not ok. Twenty minutes ago you stopped yourself when you were about to swear. Think about what you did back then and try using it in this situation.' Using the learning from these past situations, have the person repeat what they are doing successfully with the existing problem.

You Will Always Get ...

There is an old saying: 'You will always get what you've always got, if you always do what you've always done.' Albert Einstein used doing the same thing over and over again and expecting different results as the definition of insanity. If the outcome of your intervention did not achieve the desired result, then using the same intervention again is unlikely to prove any more effective the next time. If it does not work, move on to something else. You can always come back to it later if the situation changes and circumstances warrant it.

Where someone continually repeats a behaviour, using the above sayings might help stimulate their thinking. Then discuss, 'Is there another means of approaching the problem?' It then becomes a coaching strategy.

Remember to use the wisdom in this saying yourself by varying strategies if what you are trying is not working.

Overcorrection

This strategy works by having the person overcorrect their problem behaviour. Not only do those 'who overcorrect make things right with the environment or the person they've disturbed, but they make things better than they were before the disruption.' (Malott et al, 1993, p. 64). The idea is that they have to make amends for their actions but in a way that presents a larger consequence. This of course is working in the adverse conditions section of the response style curve [T] and would form a consequence.

If someone throws some rubbish on the ground, the normal consequence might be a reprimand and their having to pick up the piece of rubbish. Overcorrection would be where they have to pick up all the rubbish in the area. This might be used to increase the consequences as time goes by for each recurrence. Another example is apologising to a person. Overcorrected could mean the consequence is not only apologising personally but also publicly in front of the whole group.

You're Still Making a Statement

One of the most frustrating and difficult behaviours to deal with is total passivity, most often expressed through a passive communication style. The irony is that choosing not to communicate is actually a form of communication, so it still sends a message. Making it clear that, because they are still expressing an opinion, that they might as well make it the one they really want, can sometimes break a passive deadlock. 'Sure, not saying anything is OK but you do realise, don't you, that it seems to indicate that you agree with the others? Do you?' Or 'Not doing anything is still a form of communicating. Refusing to talk to someone tells them something is wrong but does not tell them what it is.'

Dealing with Aggression

As mentioned earlier, physical aggression and violence require special care. If you are working for a particular organisation, there may be policies and procedures in place that are relevant. Of course there is also laws to consider. Most instances following aggression may be dealt with using the strategies already discussed. The following are some additional strategies for your immediate response to control the situation.

The immediate strategy used is based on the information gained in the behaviour and emergency steps. Are they reacting or being premeditated in the aggression?

During the incident:

- *Premeditated*

When intimidation is being used, you can potentially prevent violence by not showing fear, and instead identifying clearly for the person their choices and the consequences to them resulting from those choices (San Francisco Police Academy, undated). Smith et al, (1993) advise: avoid threats, citing unrealistic or exaggerated consequences, swearing, and insults, which can all be interpreted as bluffing. Failure to communicate or being ambiguous should also be avoided. These will increase the perpetrator's perception that he or she needs to do more, which increases the situational risk.

Be clear and matter of fact when stating the consequences for an action, maintaining a detached, emotionless tone.

It may be safer to move those who are at risk away from the situation, rather than addressing the intimidator.

- *Reacting*

When dealing with people who are reacting to something through fear or frustration/anger, addressing the underlying emotion is required (San Francisco Police Academy, undated). With fear, the goal is to reduce the perceived threat. Be careful to avoid increasing any perceived threat, including via your own body language. A confident, calm and reassuring manner will assist with this (Smith et al, 1993).

Frustration or anger requires helping them to regain self-control. Again, being self-confident and calm will help. Issue repetitive instructions but avoid any threats (Smith et al, 1993). Consider using both direct responses to the person as well as taking control of the situation to defuse it.

It may be safer, if possible, to have the trigger for the emotion removed rather than working directly with the person.

After the incident:

Once the immediate response has proved effective, a strategy to deal with the causes and the long-term implications is required. When intervening between others, a conflict resolution process should be used, such as the bringing people together tool. This is primarily for use in reactive aggression. Where the aggression is premeditated, serious care needs to be taken in the resolution process. Substantial fear and/or an unequal power dynamic will disrupt the process. Professional intervention and restorative justice processes could be required in these situations.

Special care needs to also focus on the relational aspects afterwards. Ensure others are not drawn into the situation as vigilantes. The social status can change for both aggressor and victim because of the incident and should be monitored. Those involved as well as observers and other outsiders may use relationship aggression to get justice. Given the possible public nature of the incident, consider how best to publicise the resolution. Ensuring privacy is important but everyone also needs to be aware that a process has occurred and resolution reached. This can help manage the social impact while still balancing privacy issues.

Additional follow-up actions are required after a serious aggressive or violent situation and this is discussed in chapter thirteen (page 137).

Chapter twelve

Case study: Jessie and Harley

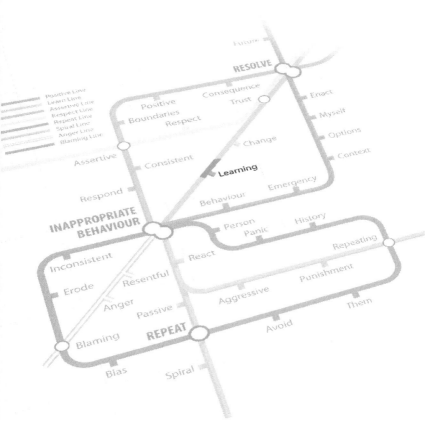

To help illustrate the many principles, tools, steps and strategies contained in this book, this chapter provides a single case study and outlines how the process can be successfully implemented.

Jessie and Harley

A group of students have finished lunch and are enjoying some free time in the sun. Some have decided to play with a soccer ball and divided themselves into two teams. Other students not involved in the game are standing nearby, watching and talking.

The ball is kicked out wide towards a group of students watching. Harley chases down the ball. Jessie seeing the ball coming leaves the group on the sideline and kicks it away from Harley. Harley watches in disbelief as the ball goes under a shrub and then confronts Jessie.

'What did you do that for, you dumb shit?' Harley shouts, shoving Jessie who nearly falls over. Jessie reddens and looks down at the ground, silent. Harley stares at Jessie, hands on hips, challenging a response.

Seeing this occur, you intervene. Harley has been physically aggressive on other occasions in the past few months. This occurs when interference by others blocks a goal or a need. Jessie is a quiet student and has no history of causing trouble. There is no prior history of conflict between Harley and Jessie. The school has a well-established behaviour agreement for all students to follow.

STEP ONE B – Behaviour

Aim:	To clearly describe the behaviour.
Action:	Identify the inappropriate behaviour and determine why it is unacceptable.

Discussion

Approaching the situation – using the principles

You approach the situation by using the underlying principles.

There are two behaviours that require addressing, each for separate people. This requires completing the steps for each person simultaneously. If you only address one of the behaviours it would not be consistent [P]. And your response would not take into account the need for different approaches for each of the behaviours. As Harley's behaviour is the most significant, it is logical to use this as the starting point.

Unconditional positive regard [P] for both Harley and Jessie is important. Given that Harley has some history of inappropriate behaviour, you may have emotions that affect your perspective. This could be that Harley is a troublemaker or frequently behaves badly. Because Jessie has no such history, this could make you feel more inclined to be biased and blame Harley for the entire incident. The test is whether you would react the same way if the behaviours were reversed and Jessie had done the shoving. It's always important to focus on the behaviour and not the personalities.

The way you deal with the situation should be that of a role model [P] to Harley, Jessie and the surrounding students, demonstrating an appropriate way to deal with the situation. Reacting [P] to the situation with an inappropriate response will not help you resolve the situation or provide the observational learning that helps encourage the desired type of behaviour.

Given that there is aggressive behaviour involved, you are justified [P] when intervening with Harley. As Jessie's behaviour has interfered with other's rights, there is also justification [P] for taking action. To not take action would indicate that it is OK to be aggressive as well as interfere with the rights of others. To maintain appropriate boundaries and ensure consistency [P], you must address both behaviours.

This situation would not have occurred if Harley and Jessie had each done things differently. Harley needs to swap [P] the physical aggression and use of a putdown with some form of assertive communication. Jessie needs to swap the method of becoming involved in the game. The possible skills [P] that might help achieve this are, for Harley, using effective communication, and for Jessie, self-control and/or the positive skills necessary to join a group.

Understanding the situation – using the tools
Using the agreement and four communication tools, you can quickly describe the behaviour.

Harley:
Reacts to having the ball kicked away by using an aggressive communication style [T]. It includes all communication channels [T] of words, tone and body. Harley is physically aggressive when shoving Jessie, yet, after the initial push, the aggression does not continue. The verbal aggression uses a putdown along with a blaming You-message [T]. This is overt reactive aggression [T]. It breaches the agreement [T] to respect others, provide constructive feedback, avoid putting others down and to act safely.

Jessie:
Interferes with the soccer game by kicking the ball away when not participating on a team. This is an aggressive communication style [T] because it interferes with the rights of others. The communication channel used is body language; no verbal comments were made. You, therefore, cannot effectively implement the I-message and You-messages tool. The interference with others' rights is a breach of the agreement [T].

The aggression type is inconclusive. The aggression is not overtly directed at a person but potentially could be relational. Kicking the ball away might be in direct response to something else Harley has done previously. It could be a relationship issue with the group playing soccer. Why Jessie interfered in the game then becomes important but remains unclear. It appears equally likely that it could either have been a spur of the moment reaction because the ball came near him, or a premeditated act. This alerts you to the need to investigate this further.

You now have a solid description and reasonable understanding of the behaviours involved.

STEP TWO   E – Emergency Assessment

Aim	Keep everyone safe.
Action	Determine if there is any danger or risk present in the situation.

Discussion
Understanding the situation – using the tools
Using the aggression risk assessment and response intensity matching tools helps evaluate the risk.

Harley:
Using the aggression risk assessment tool, you look at the E – emotional arousal, S-signs, state and symptoms and the P – past history of aggression (ESP). Emotional arousal appears to be frustration or anger directed at the interference. The reaction signals some loss of self-control. But after the initial response Harley stops and there is no verbal or physical indication that Harley will continue or increase the level of aggression.

There are no signs, symptoms or states that indicate that drugs, injury or illness are factors to consider. The past history, however, indicates aggression has occurred. The emotional arousal and history indicate risk of further aggression. You need to take action to ensure the situation does not escalate.

Given that Harley seems to have regained some self-control after the initial reaction, your response intensity [T] should aim to gain control of the situation and help calm the heightened emotions. A lower intensity than what Harley showed seems appropriate, unless you want to set a strict example.

Jessie:

The aggression risk assessment tool indicates Jessie has no significant emotional arousal when instigating the behaviour. It was not overtly directed at anyone in particular. The subsequent body language suggested by Jessie retreating is not that of someone wanting to escalate the situation. The danger is if significant fear occurs and, feeling trapped, Jessie feels there is no other option but to fight back.

Again, there are no signs, symptoms or states that would indicate drugs, injury or illness are factors to consider. Jessie's past history indicates aggression has not occurred so the only risk factor that appears present is a fear-filled emotional arousal. Given that the behaviour is of low intensity [T], it indicates you can deal with Jessie calmly; a high intensity intervention would be seen as an overreaction.

Comparing the two, Harley presents a greater risk of aggression and of higher intensity while Jessie displays a lesser potential for aggression and less intensity. You should deal with Harley's behaviour first to help ensure self-control. This has multiple benefits, including helping Harley maintain self control and providing safety to Jessie thereby reducing the likelihood of a fear-induced aggressive reaction.

STEP THREE   C – Context

Aim	Identify any other factors potentially contributing to the situation.
Action	Review the history, circumstances and situational context surrounding the behaviour.

Discussion

Approaching the situation – using the principles

As you use the tools to understand the context, consider the impact of the three biases: blaming the person, blaming the situation and blaming the victim.

Harley:
If you empathise with Harley, because Jessie's unprovoked interference leads you to think that Harley's behaviour is justified, this blames the victim [P]. As you are an independent witness to the situation, blaming the situation [P] does not become a factor. (If you were Jessie or Harley, blaming everything on the situation and taking no personal responsibility would be blaming the situation bias.) Lastly, you could concentrate the blame solely on the problem of a personal failing of Harley's and blame the person [P]. This overlooks the actual circumstances and you could then fail to recognise that Jessie also acted inappropriately.

Jessie:
There is no obvious explanation for the behaviour of Jessie having kicked the ball away. This increases the danger occurring of you blaming the person [P] as it provides an easy explanation for the behaviour. Jessie has some personality factor that wants to disrupt others' fun, you might reason. This is likely to work together with thinking that Jessie deserved the response (blaming the victim) and, so, focus more attention on Jessie's behaviour. This could leave Harley's inappropriate behaviour unchallenged.

Understanding the situation – using the tools
The three tools to use when reviewing the context are patterns, perception of the triggers and Maslow's Hierarchy of Needs.

Harley:
Using the tool designed to look for patterns we look at consistency over time, distinctiveness (of the situation, triggers and entities involved) and consensus of others behaviour. Harley's behaviour is similar to past actions of aggression having consistency over time. Past aggression occurred in situations related to where goals have been frustrated so there is no distinctiveness from that aspect. The uniqueness is that Jessie is involved and has not had previous altercations with Harley, indicating there is no other relationship issue at work. No others in the playing group reacted similarly so there is no consensus. A pattern to this behaviour

becomes evident and Harley appears to need skills in dealing with frustrating situations.

Harley has correctly identified the trigger as inappropriate behaviour (perception of trigger [T]). This means you need to support Harley in using an appropriate response. The possible need being expressed (Maslow's Needs [T]) could be: fairness and predictability (security) and/or no interference, maintaining self-esteem and respect from others (esteem). Further investigation would be required to understand the need, which might become relevant in selecting a suitable response option.

Jessie:

Jessie's behaviour is unlike past actions (there is no consistency) and is different to other situations in which Jessie has been involved (there is distinctiveness). No others in the non-playing group interfered so there is no consensus. You can conclude this behaviour is not typical of Jessie and is most likely a spur of the moment reaction.

As Jessie was the instigator, reviewing perception of the trigger [T] is not helpful. In the event that there was evidence of a pattern of behaviour, then it would help you to understand the context by reviewing the triggers for the behaviour. Repeat interference might be due to a power play to feel in control (security) or intimidate to build credibility (esteem). Alternatively it could be a clumsy attempt to join the game (belonging).

Whatever the initial need that created the trigger, this now changes, based on Harley's reaction. Jessie's needs might now focus on personal safety or self-defence (security) or to maintain respect with the group (esteem). To achieve this, Jessie might make a counter-attack, as discussed in the emergency step.

STEP FOUR   O – Options

| Aim | Begin formulating your response plan. |
| Action | Review and decide upon the most suitable style of response. |

Discussion

Approaching the situation – using the principles

Harley:

Examining Harley's behaviour for strengths (everyone has strengths [P]) may provide new information or ideas. It would then be useful to look at other appropriate behaviours that could be swapped with the inappropriate behaviour. From the information you now possess, one strength Harley has shown is his willingness to stand up for fairness and/or the right to play without interference.

With the positive reinforcement [P] principle, you would search for behaviour to encourage or reward. Standing up for one's rights is worth encouraging. And, as indicated in the behaviour step principles, swapping [P] and problems into skills [P], assertive communication is what you should reinforce.

You would try and avoid punishment [P] (consequences) wherever possible. However, considering the aggressive nature and history of the behaviour, this might not be possible or wise.

Jessie:

Given the out of character nature of Jessie's behaviour, it is unlikely that examining the strengths (everyone has strengths [P]) will provide a great deal of new information. The one positive to be gleaned from this is that Jessie has responded by choosing not to escalate the situation by retaliating with aggression.

The non-aggressive response is the only thing you can positively reinforce [P]. There are times when you cannot swap [P] the behaviour and the only option is to stop (extinguish) it. In this case, not interfering with the games of others is hard to provide a meaningful reward. You generally do not congratulate everyone regularly with, 'You're not interfering! Keep it up!' The only option is giving general feedback that lacks specific examples, such as, 'Everyone is respecting others' rights, which is great!' If the need for Jessie had been a desire to join in the game, then joining skills could be coached and positively reinforced.

The last consideration is to avoid punishment [P] wherever possible. Given that the behaviour is a minor respect issue, consequences in this scenario are unwarranted.

Understanding the situation – using the tools

Using the response style curve [T], you are now in a position to establish the style of the response required.

Harley:

The use of physical aggression requires at the very least, a reprimand and more likely the use of a specified consequence. Even though it was a reaction borne of frustration and Harley was able to regain self-control, there is the history of similar behaviour to consider. Some consequence is required. Once the initial style such as reprimand has been used, it would improve the outcome to then change to a coaching style. This would be in the form of perhaps a discussion of the appropriate ways to respond.

If this is a newly established group, you may wish to take a tough initial stance even if no history of past behaviour within the group exists. This would establish a strong group norm. It is difficult to start relaxed and then get stronger because it lacks consistency [P]. Implying that it was initially OK to do something and changing it later, creates uncertainty and leads to boundary-pushing.

Jessie:

Jessie's behaviour is not part of a demonstrated pattern; neither was it directly aggressive. A challenging style of response seems most appropriate. This will also help you gather more information as to why the behaviour occurred.

Therefore, the response styles suggested are:

Harley – Reprimand or enforce consequences and providing coaching

Jessie – Challenge

STEP FIVE   M – Myself

| Aim | Having self-awareness of the personal influence you generate. |
| Action | Assess your part in creating the context, and your ability to deliver a positive outcome. |

Discussion

Approaching the situation – using the principles

Everyone makes mistakes. This principle serves to remind you to own up to your mistakes and to admit that you can get things wrong. If you witnessed the incident, then this is minimised by the other steps, principles and tools. Be aware of jumping to conclusions if you did not view the whole event. Important details might be missing from your incomplete observation, in which case it is better to reserve judgement and gather more information.

Understanding the situation – using the tools

No matter what the situation, using the self-awareness checklist will help improve your response. Below we briefly look at all the questions posed in chapter nine (page 91).

How have I contributed to this situation?

In this case study, you are an observer. The trigger was between the two other parties, independent of you, so it is unlikely you have caused or contributed to the situation.

Am I at risk dealing with the issue?

It is unlikely there is a risk of physical aggression towards you. There would be various obligations to deal with such as organisational requirements and possibly legal requirements. You really do have to act otherwise it could create other risks.

Am I trying to impose my beliefs on the other person?

This is a clear breach of accepted behaviour guidelines and so this is not a case of imposing personal beliefs unfairly.

Do I have strong feelings about the other person?

Given Harley's past history this may affect your feelings and views regarding this incident. Be aware of these to help reduce any bias being created because of these emotions. Is Jessie so well behaved that you are prepared to overlook Jessie's part and place all the blame on Harley?

Am I the right person to implement this strategy effectively?

As you are the only person present that does make you the right person, at least for the initial response. Given that consequences may need to be used this might require referral to another person to review the incident and implement the consequences.

Do I have sufficient time and energy to devote to this?

Are you feeling tired or sick? Are there other pressing issues that you need to deal with? This could impact on the time and concentration you can apply to this issue. You may need to quickly intervene and then complete further responses later or deal with the matter to completion straight away.

What is the status of our relationship?

The assumption has been that you were a staff member supervising the students. However, the situation would change dramatically if you happen to be a visitor just walking past. What would you do? Intervene, do nothing or report it to a staff member. Will intervening do any good because you lack a relationship with Harley?

The other consideration is that you may have dealt with a number of incidents with Harley to a point where the relationship is strained. No matter what you do, it could be likely that it will be totally disregarded or make the situation worse. These aspects can only be decided on an individual case-by-case basis.

Am I and my message perceived as genuine?

If you were a visitor it is unlikely that threats of consequences will be seen as credible. Coming from a staff member they will be more genuine. As previously mentioned do not threaten consequences that cannot or will not be implemented. It will erode your credibility.

Reviewing the checklist helps provide neutrality, a key aspect to consider in your ability to form a correct and effective response. It also alerts you to other potential issues that might need to be addressed. In this example, assuming you are a staff member, there would be no impediment to completing the initial response. The issuing of consequences would need to be resolved based on the organisations policy.

STEP SIX   E – Enact

Aim	Respond to the behaviour.
Action	Implement your response strategy.

Discussion
Approaching the situation – using the principles

Harley:
It is important that you communicate clearly [P] to Harley that physical aggression and verbal abuse are not acceptable. But the trigger for the situation does actually demand a response from Harley. You cannot force Harley to do nothing (you cannot force change [P]) as that would not be respecting the rights of all parties. Providing an alternative behaviour is required.

Jessie:
Clear communication to Jessie is also required to reinforce that interfering is not respectful of the rights of others.

Responding to the situation – using the strategies
There are 20 possible strategies provided in chapter eleven (page 103) from which to draw. Combined with the tools described in the six steps like communication channels, I-messages and bringing people together, this provides a variety of ways to address the situation.

Harley:

As decided in the emergency step, Harley's behaviour should be addressed first. The response style at the option step was first to reprimand or provide consequences, and subsequently coach on appropriate behaviour. The strategy you could use is naming the behaviour: 'Harley, it is not OK to push and put down others.' Delivering this in a serious tone (communication channels), combined with physically nearing the two parties, will help take control. You would place yourself in a position where you can best secure the physical safety of both parties.

A reminder about the agreement may also be incorporated. 'We have agreed to respect each other.' These would be clear statements that the behaviour was not acceptable. With the reprimand delivered and an acknowledgement received from Harley that it was wrong, you can then move to the coaching role.

The coaching role could explain the benefits of using an I-message: 'This is a situation where an assertive I-message could have been used to get your message across'. The inevitable response from Harley will be to try and justify the behaviour with a 'Well, Jessie started it'. This can be acknowledged but delayed so you are not distracted from your plan: 'I saw what happened and I am going to speak to Jessie about that it a minute, but, at the moment, we are discussing what you did.' This way you can keep the focus on Harley until satisfactorily resolved but make it clear that Jessie has not gotten away with facing responsibility for interrupting the game.

If you are going to implement some consequences, do this after completion of the coaching role. This ensures that the appropriate behaviour message is received. Handing out consequences first will mean the parties will focus on what this means to them rather than the coaching on what they should have done. Compliance is more likely if the perception is 'If I listen to the coaching I might not suffer any consequences'. Ongoing coaching and encouragement for Harley in using I-messages should be provided.

Jessie:

After dealing with Harley, the next step is to challenge Jessie. Using a less stern and more enquiring tone, you could ask, 'Jessie, why did you kick the ball away? That is not very respectful of those playing the game.' This names [S] the behaviour and its impact and also forces Jessie to reflect on the behaviour and provide a reason. Jessie might not understand the reasoning behind what felt like a spur of the moment reaction.

By investigating, you can uncover more information that may become useful if a pattern emerges. If Jessie replies, 'I just wanted to play as well', you understand there was an underlying need of wanting to join in. A reply of 'I don't know' indicates it was spur of the moment decision and Jessie really does not know why.

It should be clear to the pair what has just occurred. There appears no need to start a formal conflict resolution (bringing people together [T]). If this incident was the culmination of some ongoing tension and incidents, then the conflict resolution procedure would be useful in helping work through the underlying issue(s).

This should resolve the issue and help maintain the expected behaviour norms established in the agreement. A summary of the BECOME steps for this case study is provided in Appendices 4 and 5.

Chapter thirteen
After the event

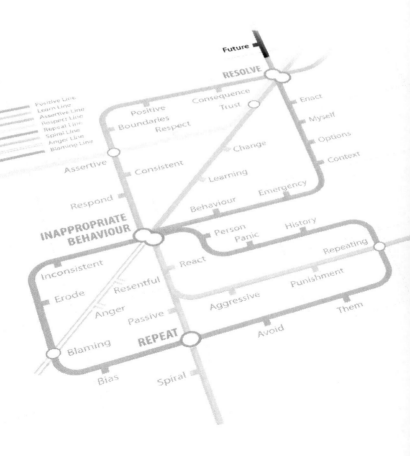

Tools in this book are designed to minimise the influence of reacting inappropriately to situations as a result of our own emotions, as this can create more problems. However, it is important to recognise the emotional impact that occurs which affects your wellbeing. Steps to deal with the emotional fallout are an important part of good practice and help prevent burnout. The following points cover caring for yourself, especially after being involved in significant incidents.

Four key actions after a major incident are reporting, supporting, defusing and debriefing (Koch and Hudson, 2000). Depending on your situation, some actions may not be applicable.

Reporting

You may need to report an incident. The who, what and how will all relate to your specific circumstances. It is very important that physical aggression and violence are reported because of the legal and safety aspects. In addition, if no action is taken, the perpetrator gets away with it. This increases the likelihood of the behaviour recurring.

Another reason to report incidents is to track them, especially in higher risk workplaces. Given that one indicator in the ESP aggression assessment is the existence of a history of aggression, it is important that this information is appropriately passed on to others who also might be at risk of aggression (Koch and Hudson, 2000). Patterns can be observed or monitored via the reporting.

Documentation

The individual circumstances will determine whether or not it is necessary to record details of incidents, such as organisational policy and procedures and legal requirements. There may be an existing incident report available in your organisation.

A record worksheet based on the BECOME framework is provided in Appendix 3, page 144. There are examples of a complete worksheet from the case study as well. This has been provided for reflection or planning when dealing with a difficult issue. Otherwise you might like to use it to actually record incidents. However, used as an incident form has practical limitations. It creates a significant amount of report writing, especially in complex situations.

If there is a large number of people involved, a large number of incidents, or one person has a range of inappropriate behaviours, it may not be feasible to record them in the format illustrated. However, using the worksheet to summarise a person's behavioural issues may work for your situation. For example, if regular agreement violations occur, you can document each of the instances. The details from the BECOME steps are added to record the overall 'situation' for a series of events.

Only you can determine how best to use this worksheet for the particular circumstances you encounter. It can, at the very least, act as a memory guide to encouraging appropriate behaviour.

Looking after yourself

Support

It is important that peer group support is sought and provided. In supporting peers beware of blaming the victim bias (see *blaming principle* in chapter seven, page 65) occurring (Koch and Hudson, 2000). It is natural not to want to think this could happen to us, therefore, we prefer to think that the victim must have done something wrong.

Defuse

Soon after a traumatic event, say, within 12 hours, it helps to defuse. This is 'to help those involved recognise that it has finished' and includes outlining 'the event, the circumstances and the effects on those involved', (Koch and Hudson, 2000 pp. 42-3). All those involved or witnessing the event should be involved in the defusing process. It is not intended as a substitute for counselling, as this would be provided if required in the debriefing phase below.

Debrief

Where the defusing process is not enough, then debriefing should occur. It 'provides an opportunity for individuals to process the event, rather than explore issues connected with the event', (Koch and Hudson, 2000 p. 43). This is a specialist area of expertise and professional assistance should be sought. Debriefing usually occurs within three to five days following the event.

It is important to look after yourself. Seek support whenever possible, as this will help you continue to encourage appropriate behaviour.

Appendices

1. List of Strategies
2. I-message additional options
3. Blank BECOME worksheet
4. Jessie and Harley case study worksheet – Harley
5. Jessie and Harley case study worksheet – Jessie
6. Aggression assessment summary
7. Reinforcement and adverse conditions background information

Additional information and forms:

- The worksheet and a range of information sheets relating to tools are available for download at www.encouraging-appropriate-behaviour.com
- Additional information including references to other helpful resources are also available at the website.

1: List of Strategies

Naming it

Living as your word

Building or eroding

Using the agreement

Swapping

Shaping

Emotions are OK

Cooling off

Humour

Timing

Owning the behaviour

Modelling

Coaching

Logical consequences

Questioning what is going on

Exceptions

You will always get...

Overcorrection

You're still making a statement

Dealing with aggression

2: I-message additional options

Further I-message examples and variations
(Adapted from eHow.com, 2011)

For those that think the basic I-message is a bit too formulaic, below are 20 additional variations to consider. It is best to keep it simple at first when starting out with I-messages by sticking with the basic scheme outlined below.

Remember the three types of information we can provide: feelings, behaviour and effect.

The basic I-message includes the feeling and the behaviour.

I feel ... (feeling) when... (behaviour)
I feel *worried* **when** *it's well after home time and there is no phone call or message.*
I feel *angry* **when** *I get told off for things when others don't.*

Possible other words to replace **feel** are: **get** and **become**

I get *concerned* **when** *I hear stories about the dangerous pranks that are played on people.*
I become *frustrated and annoyed* **when** *people say they will do something for me and then they don't.*

Or you can reverse the order:

When... (behaviour) **I feel ...** (feeling)

When *people talk about me as if I am not even there,* **I feel** *powerless and useless.*

When *I am picked on by others,* **I feel** *this rage in my gut and just want to rip something to pieces.*

Possible other words to replace **when** are: **because, as, whenever, after,** and **due to.**

I feel *hurt* **because** *no one asked me what I thought.*

I feel *frightened* **because** *of all the yelling and pushing.*

I feel *disappointed* **because** *this mess has not been cleaned up.*

I feel *humiliated* **as** *shouting at me in front of others shows a lack of respect.*

I feel *offended* **whenever** *someone uses racist language.*

I feel *suspicious* **after** *finding out that people have not told me everything.*

I feel *anxious* **due to** *the risks involved in riding a motorbike in the city.*

The basic behaviour and effect messages

I want ... (behaviour) **because...** (effect)

I want *everyone to stay away from the edge* **because** *they could fall and get seriously hurt.*

I want *everybody to be on time* **because** *we need to have this finished tomorrow.*

I need ... (behaviour) **because ...** (effect)

I need *everyone to turn up on time* **because** *we cannot serve our customers well without all our staff.*

I expect ... (behaviour) **because ...** (effect)

I expect *everyone to treat each other with basic respect* **because** *that will make it enjoyable for everyone.*

It was my understanding that ... (behaviour) **because ...** (effect)

It was my understanding that *everyone agreed not to use putdowns* **because** *it can make people feel angry or hurt.*

The complex behaviour and effect message

I think ... (behaviour + judgement) **because**... (effect)

> **I think** *telling stories that are not true about someone is unfair* **because** *others will believe the stories and not like the person for the wrong reasons.*

The complex feeling, behaviour and effect messages

I would ... (feeling) **it if** ... (behaviour) **because** ...(effect)

> **I would** *appreciate* **it if** *everyone would ring when they are late* **because** *then I can plan to have enough staff stay back and cover till they arrive.*

I would... (feeling) **it very much** (or variation) **if**... (behaviour) **because**... (effect)

> **I would** *like* **it** much *better* **if** *only one person at a time spoke* **because** *then we can all get to hear what each other has to say.*

(behaviour and effect)... **and then I feel** ... (feeling)

> *Leaving the sports gear outside all the time means it gets ruined* **and then I feel** *angry about having to spend money to replace it.*

The final option is to use a feeling and effect message.

Just be aware that, when using this type of message, the actual behaviour that is causing the problem is not included in the message. Only its effect is, so you might need a follow-up message to outline the behaviour to change.

I feel... (feeling) **because**... (effect)

> **I feel** *hurt* **because** *I didn't get to make a choice.*
> **I feel** *frightened* **because** *the situation is dangerous.*

Possible other words to replace **because** are: **as** and **due to**

> **I feel** *sad* **as** *it hurt my feelings.*
> **I feel** *horrified* **due to** *the animals being left to go hungry.*

3: BECOME 6-step worksheet

Process Steps and Principles		Tool ☑ where appropriate	Notes Person's name:	Date Completed by
B	**Behaviour**	• What agreement is being violated?		
• Unconditional positive regard		• Passive □ Assertive □ Aggressive □?		
• Positive role model		• Using an I-message □ You-message □?		
• Consistency		• Channel – words □ tone □ body language □		
• Responding, not reacting		**• Aggression:**		
• Swapping not stopping		Way? overt □ relationship □		
• Converting problems into skills		Why? reacting □ premeditated □		
• Justification				
E	**Emergency**	**• Aggression risk assessment (ESP)**		
		• Emotion:		
		• Fear (flight or fight) □		
		• Frustration (= less control/approach) □		
		• Intimidation (= in control) □		
		• Signs of drugs □,		
		• State of illness □		
		• Symptoms of injury □		
		• Past history of aggression □		
		• Response intensity?		

C	Context	

	• Blaming bias: person, situation or victim	• **Looking for patterns**
		  • Consistency of behaviour
		  • The situation distinctiveness
		  • What others are doing (consensus)
		• **Perception of trigger**
		  • Correctly identified □ – response
		  • Incorrectly identified □ – response and thought process
		• **Maslow's Needs** – addiction and disorder, physiological, safety and security, belonging and love, esteem and self-actualisation

O	Options	
	• Everyone has strengths • Positive reinforcement • Avoid punishment	**Response Style Curve** Encourage □ Coach □ Challenge □ Reinforce □ Reprimand □ Support □ Consequence □ Bribe □ Rescue □ Revenge □

M	Myself	
	• Everyone makes mistakes	• Self-awareness Checklist

E	Enact	
	• Clear communication • You cannot force change	• Communication channels • I-messages • Bringing people together conflict resolution steps

4: Case Study Worksheet: Harley

Process Steps and Principles	Tool ☑ where appropriate	Notes Person's name: HARLEY Date TODAY Completed by ME
B Behaviour	• What agreement is being violated?	Aggressive using abusive You-message containing a put-down. 'What did you do that for, you dumb shit?' Physically aggressive by pushing Jessie. Breaches behaviour agreement – respect, feedback, put downs and safety.
• Unconditional positive regard	• Passive ☐ Assertive ☐ Aggressive ☑?	
• Positive role model	• Using an I-message ☐ You-message ☑?	
• Consistency		
• Responding, not reacting	• Channel – words ☑ tone ☑ body language ☑	
• Swapping not stopping	**• Aggression:**	
• Converting problems into skills	• Way? overt ☑ relationship ☐	
• Justification	• Why? reacting ☑ premeditated ☐	
E Emergency	**• Aggression risk assessment (ESP)**	Frustrated/angry at interference. Initial response appeared instinctive and then regained self-control. ESP risk E: yes S: no P: yes – Appears likelihood of further physical interaction reduced now that has regained self control unless called to defend self. No verbal or physical indication that wanted to escalate to sustained physical aggression.

Moderate intensity aggression. |
	• Emotion:	
	• Fear (flight or fight) ☐	
	• Frustration (= less control/approach) ☑	
	• Intimidation (= in control) ☐	
	• Signs of drugs ☐,	
	• State of illness ☐	
	• Symptoms of injury ☐	
	• Past history of aggression ☑	
	• Response intensity?	

C	Context		

	• Blaming bias: person, situation or victim	• **Looking for patterns**
		  • Consistency of behaviour
		  • The situation distinctiveness
		  • What others are doing (consensus)
		• **Perception of trigger**
		  • Correctly identified ☑ – response
		  • Incorrectly identified ☐ – response and thought process
		• **Maslow's Needs** – addiction and disorder, physiological, safety and security, belonging and love, esteem and self-actualisation
			Part of group playing soccer. Was chasing after ball when Jessie who was a bystander interfered with game by kicking ball into garden. Harley has history of past aggressive behaviour. Behaviour consistent with past actions when frustrated. Distinctiveness to situation is Harley and Jessie have not had prior altercations. No consensus occurring (no others in group have shown similar behaviour).
			
			Trigger correctly identified but response inappropriate.
			
			Possible need for esteem (respect from others) and/or security (predictability and no interference).

O	Options		
	• Everyone has strengths • Positive reinforcement • Avoid punishment	**Response Style Curve** Encourage ☐ Coach ☑ Challenge ☐ Reinforce ☐ Reprimand ☐ Support ☐ Consequence ☑ Bribe ☐ Revenge ☐ Rescue ☐	Given the use of physical aggression requires reprimand/consequence. Requires coaching about appropriate ways of responding.
M	Myself		
	• Everyone makes mistakes	• Self-awareness Checklist	No relationship issues or previous history of having to deal with Harley. No other staff present.
E	Enact		
	• Clear communication • You cannot force change	• Communication channels • I-messages • Bringing people together conflict resolution steps	Addressed first. 'Harley, it is not OK to push and put-down others.' Using serious tone and moved in to take command of the space to secure physical safety. Move to coach role but still with stern tone and discuss I messages. Issue or refer to others to issue consequences.

5: Case Study Worksheet: Jessie

Process Steps and Principles		Tool ☑ where appropriate	Notes Person's name: JESSIE	Date TODAY Completed by ME
B	**Behaviour**	• What agreement is being violated?	Interfered with soccer game by kicking the ball away while not playing in a team.	
	• Unconditional positive regard	• Passive ☐ Assertive ☐ Aggressive ☑?	Aggressive – interfering with rights of others.	
	• Positive role model	• Using an I-message ☐ You-message ☐?	No verbal comments made.	
	• Consistency	• Channel – words ☐ tone ☐ body language ☑	Unsure if overt or relationship towards Harley or group.	
	• Responding, not reacting	**• Aggression:**	Possibly reaction or premeditated.	
	• Swapping not stopping	• Way? overt ☐ relationship ☐		
	• Converting problems into skills	• Why? reacting ☐ premeditated ☐		
	• Justification			
E	**Emergency**	• Aggression risk assessment (ESP)	Appears in control. Either spur of the moment or possible intimidation/power play to feel in control and build credibility with other non players in group. Stepped back when challenged indicating did not intend to respond to physical aggression with own physical response. Likelihood of further physical interaction low unless called to defend self. ESP risk: E possible fear, S no and P no.	
		• Emotion:		
		• Fear (flight or fight) ☑		
		• Frustration (= less control/approach) ☐		
		• Intimidation (= in control) ☐		
		• Signs of drugs ☐,	Minor issue – low intensity response.	
		• State of illness ☐		
		• Symptoms of injury ☐		
		• Past history of aggression ☐		
		• Response intensity?		

C	**Context**	Group playing soccer while Jessie and others looked on. Jessie kicked the ball into garden when it came near. Harley who was running for the ball verbally abused and pushed Jessie. Jessie stepped back and did not engage Harley and acted surprised at the aggressive response. Has not displayed this type of behaviour before (no consistency and is distinctive) and no one else attempting to do similar (consensus). No past behaviour issues.
	• **Looking for patterns** 　• Consistency of behaviour 　• The situation distinctiveness 　• What others are doing (consensus) • **Perception of trigger** 　• Correctly identified □ – response 　• Incorrectly identified □ – response and thought process • **Maslow's Needs** – addiction and disorder, physiological, safety and security, belonging and love, esteem and self-actualisation	Jessie was the instigator. Appeared to be spur of the moment action. Possible need to feel in control (security) through intimidation and/or build credibility (esteem). Or wanting to join the game (belonging). Reaction to aggression might focus on personal safety or self-defence (security) or maintain respect with the group (esteem).
	• Blaming bias: person, situation or victim	
O	**Options**	Given it is unpatterned behaviour, challenge toward Jessie most appropriate.
	• Everyone has strengths • Positive reinforcement • Avoid punishment **Response Style Curve** Reinforce □　Encourage □　Coach □　Challenge ☑　Reprimand □ Support □ Bribe □　Consequence □ Rescue □　Revenge □	
M	**Myself**	No relationship issues or previous history of having to deal with Jessie. No other staff present.
	• Everyone makes mistakes • Self-awareness Checklist	
E	**Enact**	After dealing with Harley's behaviour asked Jessie 'Why did you kick the ball away? That was not very respectful of those playing the game? Complete discussion about respect for others.
	• Clear communication • You cannot force change • Communication channels • I-messages • Bringing people together conflict resolution steps	

6: Aggression assessment summary
(Adapted from San Francisco Police Academy (undated) and Arraij (2010))

Category	Item	Description and examples	Risk		
			LOW		HIGH
E Emotional arousal	Fear	Being fearful creates need to move away to avoid (flight response) unless feeling trapped and having no other option but to attack to protect self.	No fear	Some fearfulness but does not interfere with social interactions	Significant fear, or fear that interferes with social interactions
	Frustration	Frustration and anger caused by interference or disruption of goal. Moves to confront source (fight response).	No frustration	Some frustration but does not interfere with social interactions	Significant frustration that does interfere with social interactions
	Intimidation	Unemotional and lacks empathy. Feels justified in using threats to achieve goal.	No intimidation		Intimidation present

Category	Item	Description and examples	Risk LOW			Risk HIGH
	Drug	*Delirium:* temporary change in brain chemistry, e.g., intoxication states, psychoactive drug withdrawal states, insulin shock (low blood sugar). Correlation between substance abuse and violence	No drugs/delirium	Somewhat altered but doesn't interfere with social interactions		Significant delirium, or delirium that does interfere with social interactions
S Signs, state and symptoms	Illness	*Decompensation:* Periods when a person with a serious mental illness is in a psychotic state. Correlation between decompensation and violence is more robust with certain diagnoses, e.g., chronic paranoid schizophrenia and bipolar affective disorder.	No mental illness/decompensation	Somewhat decompensated but at or near baseline		Significant decompensation or below baseline
	Injury	*Dementia:* Permanent change in a person's brain structure associated with confusion or higher rate of disruptive and potentially dangerous behaviour, e.g., Alzheimer's disease and AIDS-related dementia, temporal lobe epilepsy, traumatic brain injuries (head injury or heat stroke)	No injury/dementia	Some dementia but at baseline		Significant dementia or below baseline
P Past history	Violence	History and recent occurrences of violence in family of origin or has committed actual violence	No history of violence	Violence in family of origin or violent more than 6 months prior (past history)		Violence in family of origin or violent within last 6 months (recent)

The more risk items present the higher the risk. The more significant the presentation of each or any of the individual risk items the higher the risk.

7: Reinforcement and adverse conditions background information

(Adapted from Malott, Whaley and Malott, 1993)

In step four, Options (chapter eight), when discussing the response options curve [T], it was mentioned that this curve was developed from the work of behavioural psychologists such as Skinner and his operant conditions. The difficulty with use of this work is the complex way it is explained, in particular the use of technical terms. This overview is not to try and replicate the information provided in numerous texts but to provide a short overview of some of the key themes.

To break it down into its parts, there are three themes:

1. There are two types of behaviours which for our purposes can be labelled either appropriate or inappropriate.
2. There are two types of responses to the behaviour which are known as conditions. These are reinforcers and adverse conditions. Definitions for these two terms are below.
3. There are two possible options when using reinforcers or adverse conditions. You can either add or remove them.

From this there are eight possibilities to any situation. Any behaviour is either appropriate or inappropriate to which we can add or remove either a reinforcer or an adverse condition. This can all be summarised in the following diagram, which also provides some examples.

Behavioural psychology summary

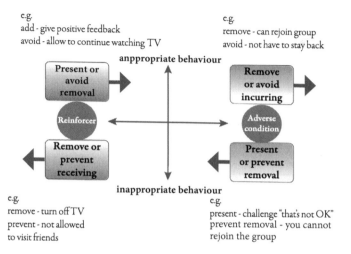

e.g.
add - give positive feedback
avoid - allow to continue watching TV

e.g.
remove - can rejoin group
avoid - not have to stay back

anppropriate behaviour

Present or avoid removal

Remove or avoid incurring

Reinforcer

Adverse condition

Remove or prevent receiving

Present or prevent removal

inappropriate behaviour

e.g.
remove - turn off TV
prevent - not allowed to visit friends

e.g.
present - challenge "that's not OK"
prevent removal - you cannot rejoin the group

Definitions:

Reinforcer – 'A stimulus, event, or condition that will increase the future likelihood of a response if it immediately follows the behaviour' (Malott et al. 1993, p. 6). You therefore present (add) or avoid removing the reinforcer for appropriate behaviour while you remove or prevent recieving the reinforcer for inappropriate behaviour. This has a strong relationship to satisfying needs.

Adverse Condition – 'An adverse condition is one we tend to minimise contact with', (Malott et al. 1993, p. 37). You therefore present (add) or prevent removing the adverse condition for inappropriate behaviour while you remove or avoid incurring the adverse condition for appropriate behaviour.

Reference list

Anderson, Craig A. and Bushman, Brad J. (2002) *Human Aggression*. Annual Review Psychology 2002. 53:27–51

Arrajj, Mike (2010) *A Typology for Interpersonal Violence* http://www.nhchc.org/2_2010TypologyInterpersonalViolence_ Mike%20Arrajj.pdf (accessed 18/02/2011)

Baldwin, John D. and Baldwin, Janice I. (1998) *Behaviour Principles in Everyday Life*, 3rd ed. Upper Saddle River, New Jersey, USA: Prentice-Hall

Cornelius, Helena and Faire, Shoshana. (2006). *Everyone Can Win: Responding to Conflict Constructively*. Pymble NSW, Australia: Simon & Schuster

Coyne, Sarah M., Archer, John and Eslea, Mike (2006) *"We're Not Friends Anymore! Unless": The Frequency and Harmfulness of Indirect, Relational, and Social Aggression* AGGRESSIVE BEHAVIOR Volume 32, pages 294 –307

eHow (2011) *How to use I messages, solve conflicts*. http://www.ehow. com/how_5797583_use-_i-messages_-solve-conflicts.html (accessed 24/4/2011)

Field, Evelyn M. (1999) *Bully Busting: How to help children deal with teasing and bullying*. Lane Cove NSW, Australia: Finch Publishing

Fung, Annis Lai-Chu, Raine, Adrian and Gao, Yu. (2009) Cross-Cultural Generalizability of the Reactive–Proactive Aggression Questionnaire (RPQ) *Journal of Personality Assessment*, 91(5), 473–479

Furman, Ben. (2004) *Kids' Skills: Playful and practical solution-finding with children*. Bendigo Vic, Australia: St Luke's Innovative Resources

Gibbs, Jeanne. (1994). *Tribes: A New Way of Learning Together*. Santa Rosa, CA: Center Source Publications

Gilligan, Stephen G. (1999) *Therapeutic Trances: The Cooperation Principle in Ericksonian Hypnotherapy*. Levittown, PA, USA: Brummer/Mazel

Hickson III, Mark, Stacks, Don W. and Moore, Nina-Jo. (2004). *Nonverbal Communication: Studies and Applications*. 4th ed. Los Angeles, California: Roxbury Publishing

Johnson, David W. and Johnson, Frank P. (1994). *Joining Together Group Theory and Group Skills* 5th ed. Needham Heights, MA, USA. Allyn and Bacon

Kassinove, Howard and Tafrate, Raymond, Chip. (2002). *Anger Management: The Complete Treatment Guidebook for Practitioners*. Atascadero, California: Impact Publishers

Kelley, Harold H. (1967). Attribution theory in social psychology. *Nebraska Symposium on motivation*, 15, 192-241 and (1973) The processes of causal attribution. *American Psychologist*, 28. 107–28, cited in Weiten, Wayne. 4th ed. (1998) *Psychology Themes and Variations*. Santa Clara University: Brooks/Cole

Koch, Tina and Hudson, Sally. (2000) *Preventing Workplace Violence: Towards a Best Practice Model for Work in the Community – Final Report*. Glenside, South Australia: Royal District Nursing Service (RDNS) RESEARCH UNIT (SA) downloaded www.safework.sa.gov.au/contentPages/docs/agedViolenceBestPractice.pdf (accessed 15 June 2011)

Lange, Arthur J. and Jakubowski, Patricia (1976). *Responsible Assertive Behavior: Cognative/Behavioral Procedures for Trainers*. Champaign, Illinois: Research Press

Little, Todd D.; Jones, Stephanie M.; Henrich, Christopher. C. and Hawley, Patricia H. (2003) Disentangling the 'whys' from the 'whats' of aggressive behaviour. *International Journal of Behaviorial Development* 2003, 27 (2), pp122–33

Luckner, John L., and Nadler, Reldan S. (1997) *Processing The Experience Strategies to Enhance and Generalize Learning*. 2nd ed. Montecito, CA: Kendall/Hunt Publishing Company

Maslow, A. H. (1970). *Motivation and personality* 2nd ed. New York: Harper and Row cited in Rathus, Spencer. A. (2004) *Psychology: Concepts and Connections Brief Version* (7th ed.) Belmont, CA, USA: Wadsworth/Thompson Learning

Malott, R.W., Whaley, D.L., and Malott, M.E. (1993) *Elementary Principles of Behaviour* 2nd ed. Englewood Cliffs, New Jersey: Prentice Hall

Mayhew, Claire. (2000) *Preventing client-initiated violence*. Australian Institute of Criminology Research and Public Policy, Series No. 30, Australian Institute of Criminology Canberra downloaded http://aic.gov.au/ (accessed 11 July 2011)

McKay, Matthew, Davis, Martha and Fanning, Patrick. (1983) *Messages: The Communication Skills Book*. Oakland, CA. New Harbinger Publications

McWhirter, J. Jeffries, McWhirter, Benedict T., McWhirter, Anna M., McWhirter, Ellen Hawley. (1998) *At-Risk Youth: A Comprehensive Response for Counselors, Teachers, Psychologists, and Human Service Professionals*. Pacific Grove, CA. Brooks/Cole Publishing Company

Plous, Scott. (1993). *The Psychology of Judgment and Decision Making*. New York: McGraw-Hill Inc.

Priest, Simon, and Gass, Michael A. (1997). *Effective Leadership in Adventure Programming*. Champaign, IL: Human Kinetics

Reber, Arthur S. (1995) *Dictionary of Psychology*. 2nd Ed. London: Penguin

Reeve, Johnmarshall. (1992) *Understanding Motivation and Emotion*. University of Rochester, River Campus: Harcourt Brace College Publishers

San Francisco Police Academy. (undated) Learning domain 37: Persons with disabilities. *New Recruit Training Manual*. San Francisco: San Francisco Police Academy cited in Arrajj, Mike (2010) *A Typology for Interpersonal Violence* http://www.nhchc.org/2_2010TypologyInterpe rsonalViolence_Mike%20Arrajj.pdf (accessed 18/02/2011)

Schoel, Jim, Prouty, Dick, and Radcliffe, Paul. (1988) *Islands of Healing: A Guide to Adventure Based Counseling*. Hamilton, MA, USA: Project Adventure

Smith, Paul A., Fox, Lorraine, Johnson, Lois, Nihart, Mary Ann, Schindler, Mark, Smiar, Nick, Reid, Glenys V., Sheahan, Clare and Sheahan, Peter. (1993) *Professional Assault Response Training Revised Australia Version*. North Ringwood, Vic: Professional Group Facilitators Pty. Ltd.

Spanovic, Marija, Lickel, Brian, Denson, Thomas F. and Petrovic, Nebosjsa. (2010). *Fear and anger as predictors of motivation for intergroup aggression: Evidence from Serbia and Republika Srpska*. Group Processes and Intergroup Relations

St Luke's Innovative Resources. (1998). *Principles of Solution-Focused Practice*

Typo Station. a) (undated, circa 2002), *Tools for your Toolbox – Introduction to Typo Station Approaches – Supporting all people to take a consistent approach*. Chesthunt, Victoria, Typo Station – (Notes: 1.

Unpublished manual for family and supporters, 2. Typo Station is now known as 'Evolve')

Typo Station. b) (undated, circa 2002), *Typo Station Living Agreement*. Chesthunt, Victoria, Typo Station – (Notes: Unpublished)

Typo Station. c) (undated), youth work principle used by staff [source unknown]

The Victorian Association for Restorative Justice. (2011) *Restorative Practices in Education* http://www.varj.asn.au/rp/education.htm (accessed 21/04/11)

Weiten, Wayne. 4th ed. (1998) *Psychology Themes and Variations*. Santa Clara University: Brooks/Cole

Index

About the author

Murray grew up in Western Australia and his first career was in banking. After 13 years he gave up being a commercial finance manager to pursue his love for the outdoors. Completing a Diploma of Recreation with Swinburne University in Victoria, he has since spent most of the past 13 years working with young people as a youth worker and educator.

As an outdoor educator Murray led week long bushwalking, rafting and canoeing expeditions with school groups, teaching outdoors skills along with environmental awareness, leadership and personal development. He has worked for the Outdoor Education Group, Evolve and Geelong Grammar – Timbertop.

Fascinated by the therapeutic aspects of outdoor adventure led Murray to working with at-risk youth. He credits the four years at Youth Enterprise Trust (YET) and Typo Station for much of the practical knowledge that forms the basis of this book. The work was intense.

A remote cattle property in Queensland was the base for YET's 14-day residential program, with Typo Station's 20-day residential program including a nine-day hike in remote areas of Victoria, of which Murray is a veteran of many expeditions. Spending days on end with groups of adolescents confronting issues was rewarding but challenging. In 2005 he began documenting what he had learnt about changing behaviours.

Murray worked for the Brotherhood of St Lawrence, twice being a team leader for six-month long workplace skills training programs. Supporting 10 young adults to gain workplace skills and experience tested his abilities in group management at times, as they completed projects like fencing, weed removal and tree planting.

Concerned about environmental issues, he worked for Environment Victoria (EV), a not-for-profit organisation running behaviour change programs. At EV he worked with local communities and groups to promote behaviours that reduced water and energy use. Drawing on his past experiences, he taught applied learning certificate students leadership skills and sustainable behaviours.

Murray later took on a senior management role overseeing all of their community education and behaviour change programs for groups as diverse as seniors, low income families, recently arrived refugees and multicultural communities.

He continues to freelance on outdoor programs for a variety of organisations. When not outdoors hiking or paddling a river, he enjoys reading non-fiction. Murray's most recent major adventure was two-months trekking and kayaking in Nepal. He currently lives in Melbourne.

To find out more visit www.encouraging-appropriate-behaviour.com

For those readers who would like to offer feedback or suggest other strategies and tools they have used, please visit the above website.

Printed in Great Britain
by Amazon.co.uk, Ltd.,
Marston Gate.